Trifles for the Christmas

H. S. Armstrong

Alpha Editions

This edition published in 2024

ISBN : 9789362090881

Design and Setting By
Alpha Editions
www.alphaedis.com
Email - info@alphaedis.com

As per information held with us this book is in Public Domain.
This book is a reproduction of an important historical work. Alpha Editions uses the best technology to reproduce historical work in the same manner it was first published to preserve its original nature. Any marks or number seen are left intentionally to preserve its true form.

Contents

THE OVERTURE. ....- 1 -
A CHRISTMAS MELODY ....- 4 -
   The Prelude. ....- 4 -
   The Refrain. ....- 7 -
   The Air. ....- 9 -
STORY OF A BEAST. ....- 11 -
LEAVES IN THE LIFE OF AN IDLER. ....- 19 -
   Leaf the First. ....- 19 -
   Leaf the Second. ....- 22 -
   Leaf the Third. ....- 24 -
   Leaf the Fourth. ....- 25 -
   Leaf the Last. ....- 29 -
MR. BUTTERBY RECORDS HIS CASE.[A] ....- 32 -
FOOTNOTES: ....- 42 -
DIAMONDS AND HEARTS. ....- 43 -
   A Sketch of Rio de Janeiro. ....- 43 -
   CHAPTER I. ....- 43 -
   CHAPTER II. ....- 45 -
   CHAPTER III. ....- 47 -
   CHAPTER IV. ....- 49 -
   CHAPTER V. ....- 53 -

THE OVERTURE.

Christmas! What worldly care could ever lessen the joy of that eventful day? At your first waking in the morning, when you lie gazing in drowsy listlessness at the brass ornament on your bed-tester, when the ring of the milkman is like a dream, and the cries of the bread-man and newspaper-boy sound far off in the distance, it peals at you in the laughter and gay greetings of the servants in the yard. Your senses are aroused by a promiscuous discharging of pistols, and you are filled with a vague thought that the whole city has been formed into a line of skirmishers. You are startled by a noise on the front pavement, which sounds like an energetic drummer beating the long roll on a barrel-head; and you have an indistinct idea that some improvident urchin (up since the dawn) has just expended his last fire-cracker.

At length there is a stir in the room near you. You hear the patter of little feet on the stairs, and the sound of childish voices in the drawing-room. What transports of admiration, what peals of joyous clamor, fall on your sleepy ears! The patter on the stairs sounds louder and louder, the ringing voices come nearer and nearer; you hear the little hands on your door-knob, and you hurry on your dressing-gown; for it is Christmas morning.

What a wonderful time you have at breakfast! There are a half-dozen silver forks for ma, a new napkin-ring for you, and what astonishing hay-wagons and crying dolls for the children! Jane, the house-maid, is beaming with happiness in a new collar and black silk apron; and Bridget will persist in wearing her silver thimble and carrying her new work-basket, though they threaten utter destruction to the beefsteak-plate.

You sit an unusually long time over your coffee that morning, and say an unusual number of facetious things to everybody. You cover Jane with confusion, and throw Bridget into an explosion of mirth, by slyly alluding to a blue-eyed young dray-man you one evening noticed seated on the kitchen steps. Perhaps you venture a prediction on the miserable existence he is some day destined to experience,—when a look from the little lady in the merino morning-wrapper checks you, and you confess to yourself that you are feeling uncommonly happy.

At last the breakfast ends, and the children go out for a romp. Perhaps you are a little taken aback when you are informed your easy-chair has been removed to the library; but you see Bridget, still in secure possession of her thimble and work-basket, with a huge china bowl in one hand and an egg-beater in the other, looking very warm and very much confused, and you take your departure to your own domain, to con over the morning papers.

You hear an indistinct sound of the drawing of corks and beating of eggs; of a great many dishes being taken out of the china-closet, and a good many orders being given in an undertone,—why is it women always will speak in a whisper when there is a man about the house?—and you lose yourself in the "leader," or the prices current.

The skirmishers have evidently suffered disaster; for the firing becomes more and more distant, and at length dies from your hearing. You are favored with a call from the improvident little boy, who requests you to grant him the privilege of collecting such of his unexploded fire-crackers as may be in your front yard, giving you, at the same time, the interesting information that they are to be made into "spit-devils." You are overwhelmed by a profound bow from the grocer's lad as he passes your window, and you invite him in and beg that he will honor you by accepting half a dollar and a handful of doughnuts:—the lady in the merino morning-wrapper has provided a cake-basket full for the occasion. You are also waited on by the milkman, who, you are glad to see, is really flesh and blood, and not, as you have sometimes supposed, an unearthly bell-ringer who visited this sublunary sphere only at five A.M., and then for the sole purpose of disturbing your morning nap. You are also complimented by the wood-man and wood-sawyer, an English sailor with a wooden leg, who once nearly swamped you in a tornado of nautical interjections, on your presenting him a new pea-jacket. And then comes the German fruit-woman, whose first customer you have the distinguished honor to be, and who, in consequence, has taken breakfast in your kitchen for the last ten years. You remember that on one occasion she spoke of her little boy, named Heinderich, who was suffering with his teeth; and when you hope that Heinderich is better, you are surprised to learn that he is quite a large boy, going to the public school, and that the lady in the merino morning-wrapper has just sent him a new cap.

The heaping pile of doughnuts gradually lessens, until finally there is not one left. The last dish is evidently taken from the china-closet, and the whole house is filled with that portentous stillness which causes the mothers of mischievous offspring so much trepidation.

You expect to see the merino morning-wrapper reconnoitering the movements of your own sweet pledges of affection; but she doesn't: you can only hear the ticking of the little French clock on the mantle-piece, and the spluttering of the coal as it bursts into a gassy flame between the bars of the grate, and you almost imagine Christmas has passed. You are deceived; for by-and-by you hear your children's footsteps as they skip over the garden-walk, and the sound of their ringing laughter as they rush in out of the cold, and their clamor rises louder and gladder and more jubilant than ever. Grandpa! Who does not know him, with his joyous face and hearty morning greeting? How resplendent he looks in his broadcloth suit, his gold-headed cane and great blue overcoat! What quantities of almonds and raisins, of oranges and sweetmeats, those overcoat-pockets contain! What child ever lived who did not believe grandpa's pocket a cornucopia for all juvenile desires? The day passes on. The turkey never looked browner or juicier, and the blaze on the pudding-sauce never burned bluer; the kissing under the mistletoe was never more delightful, nor the blindman's-buff ever played with a greater zest: but the merriest Christmas must end. Your little girl, tired and sleepy, kneels at your feet, and you pass your fingers through her soft curls, while she repeats her simple prayer: "God bless pa, God bless ma, God bless grandpa, God bless little brother, and God bless Santa Claus;" and you hope that God *will* bless Santa Claus. You thank your Creator you *are* the master of that quiet home and the father of those dear children, and go to your rest with a heart full of gratitude. You hope that all the newspaper-boys, and all the milkmen and bread-men's children, and all the little boys and girls who have no fathers or mothers or grandpas, and all the poor, and all the sick, and all the blind, and all the distressed, have had a merry Christmas.

At a time like this, when the security of your own reward relaxes scrutiny for the shortcomings of others, I would have you take up these "*Trifles.*"

A CHRISTMAS MELODY.

The Prelude.

"Twenty-nine dollars! Very well, Mr. John Redfield: I think you *have* cut your allowance a *little* low. With bracelets, bonbons, and other gewgaws for your interesting friends, I must say your enjoyment of this prospective Twenty-fifth of December is somewhat reduced. When a man has skated over the frozen surface of society a little matter of one-and-thirty years, it is just reasonable to hope he has reached that desideratum known as years of discretion. There is a little adage relating to the immeasurably short time the feeble-minded enjoy pecuniary advantages, which I think decidedly applicable to you.

"A rather severe epigram, occurring in the Holy Scriptures, goes to show the impossibility—even though the somewhat unsatisfactory argument of the pestle and mortar be resorted to—of separating the same class of people from their rather confused ideas of the fitness of things. However, when the Mussulman, careering over Sahara, finds himself, by a stumble of his horse, rolling in the sand, with his yataghan, pistols, and turban scattered around him, he rises quietly, and exclaims, 'Allah is great!' I know a Christian would have expended his wrath in a variety of anathemas highly edifying, and close by wishing his unfortunate steed in a much warmer climate than the Mohammedan has any idea of. I am a poor church-man: let me emulate the philosophy of the simple child of the desert, and when I fall into trouble bear it patiently.

"I wonder what the grim savage would do were he short of money in a land thronging with beggars and other blissful adjuncts of civilization? Woe unto every blind or club-foot man, and every one-armed or scalded woman, *I* meet to-day! They shall work out their own salvation with fear and trembling, or I'm an idiot.

"Why, bless my soul, the fortunes bequeathed to all the novel-heroes created this century, would not begin to supply them!"

Redfield shook his head decidedly when he came to this part of his monologue, and put the gold and silver coins back into his pocket.

"I hate poor people—I positively do! I despise their pale faces and cadaverous expression. I detest straggling little girls who come up to you and say their mothers have been bedridden for three months, and all their little brothers and sisters are down with the fever. I know it's a lie. I can detect at once the professional whine, and am certain the story has been repeated by rote a hundred times that day; but for the life of me I cannot put out from my mind the imaginary picture of the half-furnished room in some filthy back street, with a forlorn woman with red hair stretched on a bed of straw, and half a dozen or more red-haired children piled about promiscuously.

"There is a wretched little German girl, always managing to have a boil either on her forehead or the back of her neck,—I believe in my soul it's from overfeeding,—who follows my footsteps like a misanthropic vampire. By what ingenuity she manages to cajole me out of my money I know not, but I positively assert that in the last fortnight, according to her account, her unhappy mother has suffered from eleven different incurable diseases. My God! what a complication of misfortune! Why not let them starve? When a man is not capable of maintaining a family, why in Heaven's name does he ever have one?

"I think I will follow the maxims of political economists and all respectable members of society, and vote beggars a nuisance. I wonder how many people to-day, praying for deliverance by Christ's 'agony and bloody sweat,' by his 'cross and passion,' his 'precious death and burial,' his 'glorious resurrection and ascension,' and the 'coming of the Holy Ghost,' don't?

"This *is* a charitable frame of mind to precede a Christmas morning. When did I contract the habit of talking to myself?

"I must be impressed with the two grand reasons of the man we all know of: first, I like to talk to a sensible man, and second, I like to hear a sensible man talk.

"I wonder if there is not something under the surface in Sol Smith's charity sermon? I rather like its pithy style:

"'He that giveth to the poor, lendeth to the Lord. Now, brethren, if you are satisfied with the security, down with the dust.'

"I once repeated it to a gaunt little parson, and his look of unmitigated horror caused me to hide my diminished head. I knew from his manner—he did not condescend a reply—what chamber in the Inferno was being heated up for my especial benefit. Well, well! the sentiment is doubtless creditable to his head and heart.

"What a pity it is I am not one of the 'good' people! What an agonizingly cerulean expression I would wear, to be sure!

"I wonder why young mothers don't write for their children's first copy Dante's inscription, and teach their baby lips to lisp of the world what he says of hell. It's surprising to me that that parson is not crazed at his sense of the certain perdition into which everybody except himself is hurrying. Perhaps, after all, there is something in the question of La Rochefoucauld, 'Is it not astonishing that we are not altogether overpowered at the misfortunes of our friends?' Well, man learns something every day. When I first saw a chicken take a billful of water and hold up its head, in my childish simplicity I imagined it thanking God: I afterward discovered it was only letting the water run down its throat. My mind, like good wine or bad butter, must be strengthening by age.

"Why can't we take things quietly, as we did when we were boys? I expect I had a rather comfortable time of it then, though I did get whipped for tearing my clothes, and killing flies, which I used to do worse than any bald hornet.

"Now, that youngster walking before me is whistling like a lark, and, by the Lord Harry, he has scarcely a shoe to his foot!"

He was a poor boy, perhaps seven or eight years old. His face was pale and careworn, and though he whistled, it was a solemn kind of whistle, that sounded more like a lamentation than the outburst of childish gladness. His clothes were too thin and worn for his slight frame, for the morning, though clear and bright, was frosty, and his little bare toes peeping out of his shoes were blue with the cold. He hurried through the streets with a bundle of papers, but, even while intent on their sale, he had the walk of an old man, and his small shoulders stooped as though they bent under the weight of years.

Redfield eyed him narrowly.

"Paper, sir?"

"So, in this frenzied struggle after bread, you are an itinerant vendor of periodical literature?"

"You mean I sell papers, sir? Yes. I've only been at it three weeks. I'm 'stuck' this morning. Haven't got a good beat yet. Paper, sir?"

"Have you no fears of risking your commercial character by appearing on the streets in that unheard-of dress?"

The boy reddened.

"I've been sick," said he, at length, "for a very long time."

"My Lord!" groaned the philosopher; "here's another conspiracy against my unfortunate pocket-book! Why don't your mother take care of you?"

"She did, sir; but she sews for slop-shops, and has worked so much at night that she's almost blind."

"Worse and worse! and here's an outfitting establishment just across the street. When will I acquire anything like habits of prudence? Boy," said he, fiercely, "you are a young vagabond, and deserve to starve. Your mother should be put in the pillory for ever marrying. That's what the world says,— and what I would think, if I wasn't a consummate ass. Were you ever blessed with a view of the most unmitigated simpleton the sun ever shone upon? Look at me! Look good: I am worthy of a close inspection. Now come along, and see to what extent my folly sometimes carries me."

He caught the boy roughly by the arm, jerked rather than led him across the street, and thrust him bodily among a crowd of astonished clerks who stood at the door of a clothing-house.

"Take this young vagrant and put him into new boots, with woolen socks, some kind of a gray jacket and trowsers, and a hat that's fit for a civilized age."

Seeing that Redfield was really in earnest, the proprietor obeyed the order promptly, and in half an hour the boy reappeared, rather red, a little uncertain, but decidedly altered for the better.

"Now go," cried the cynic, with a smile, and a shake of his hand, "and thank your stars the fool-killer did not come along before you."

"Nineteen dollars and a half! Bless me! what am I coming to? It may be laying up treasures in heaven; but, by Jove, I had rather see it than hear tell of it."

The Refrain.

It certainly was the dreariest 24th of December an unhappy boy ever had the misery of witnessing. In a vain endeavor to get up an excitement, I expended my last fire-cracker; but the continuous drizzle drowned out every one. It was only four o'clock, and yet the fog hung like a pall over the windows, and the gas-men were lighting the lamps in the street. My mother, and an old schoolmate, Mrs. Mary Morton, adjourned to the privacy of her bedroom; and, a pet navigation enterprise, conducted in the gutter, having resulted in shipwreck and a severe sore throat, I also was permitted to enjoy its cosey quiet. John Redfield came in as the evening advanced. He had been sick; and my mother, wheeling the lounge near the fire, made him lie down and have something warm to drink. He and Mrs. Morton were intimate with the family from my earliest recollection.

The four, in their childhood, lived near each other, among the picturesque hills of Western Pennsylvania. They went to the same school, played in the same woods, and now, in mature life, retained the warm regard of the days gone by. I say four; for Mr. Redfield had a sister,—Mrs. Hague, a pale, lovely little lady, who at one time visited my mother very often. There had been some estrangement between her and her brother, the particulars of which I never knew. She had married, years before, a worthless kind of a man, who kept a shoestore; but he became involved, the store was sold out by the sheriff and since then both were in a manner lost.

John Redfield, though an abrupt man, and rather eccentric, had as kind a heart as any one I ever knew. He was connected with a newspaper in the city, and wrote wonderful articles about police courts, that, somehow, sounded more like sermons than stories. In my early days, before Gutenberg and his movable types came within the scope of my knowledge, I believed he printed out the whole edition with a lead-pencil, and entertained most exalted ideas of his capacity. He had a passion for giving boys painted boats. I must have received twenty—all exactly alike—at various outbreaks of his generosity. He had the queerest way of bestowing favors I almost ever saw. When he wished to make a boy a present, he shoved it roughly into his pocket, and then started off as if the house was on fire. What brought up the subject I do not now remember, but that evening Mrs. Morton persisted in talking about Clara Hague. She spoke of their childhood, of the old homestead, of the nutting, the apple-picking, the cider-making, and the hundred other occupations and amusements of their young life.

She had a vivid power of description, and a charming simplicity in her choice of words, that entertained even me; but I could see Mr. Redfield was troubled. He moved restlessly on the lounge, and once drew a shawl over his face. At last she touched on the shoestore, its doleful decay and downfall, and the years the unhappy woman had struggled on. At this he started to go; but there was something in her manner that detained him. Her tone had been light and chatty before; and, though she spoke with proper gravity, it was sprightly rather than earnest. I did not notice any striking change; and yet it seemed suddenly to assume the gentle impressiveness one sometimes fancies we should hear from the pulpit.

"Whatever be her troubles, Clara has been a good sister to you. You were the youngest; and a puny little fellow you were then, with all your greatness. Many and many a time, in your quarrels with other boys, have I seen her get into no end of disgrace for defending you. Do you *remember* that old log school-house, John? and our dinners under the trees? What baskets of berries and bags of nuts we gathered in those woods! Do you remember the little run we used to cross, and the fish you caught in the pool?

"And oh, John! do you remember that day we started home when it rained? You had been sick, and commenced to cry. We got under a big tree; but it was November; the leaves had all blown down, and the rain beat through the branches. What disconsolate little people we were! And when you sat down on a flat stone, and declared you'd stay there and die, don't you remember how Clara went out in the bushes, and, taking off her little flannel petticoat, put it around your shoulders for a cloak?"

The strong man quivered; his face convulsed, and the hot tears started into his eyes.

"YES! *I'll be hanged if I don't!*"

He clutched up his hat, and was gone in an instant, and the two women, woman-like, stood sobbing in each other's arms.

The Air.

The thousand-and-one young gentlemen in blue neck-ties, who for a twelvemonth, in frantic strains, varying from *basso profundo* to piping tenor, had proclaimed their entire willingness to "*mourir pour la patrie*," were engrossed at their shops; innumerable fascinating trimmers of bonnets, who, like poor little "Dora," religiously believed the chief end of man consisted in "dancing continually ta la ra, ta la ra," sat busily plying the needle, elbow-deep in ribbons; the consumptive-looking flute-player before the foot-lights trilled out his spasmodic trickle of melody, and contemplated with melancholy pleasure the excited audience; the lank danseuse ogled and smirked at it behind them, and, with passionate gestures of her thin legs, implored its applause; men, women, and children, of all grades and degrees, crowded into the murky night; for a day was coming when the youths of the neck-ties would not agree to *mourir* on any account; when the flute-player would cease to be contemplative; when the danseuse would forget her attenuated extremities; when the whole world, where the grace of the Redeemer is known, would believe that the chief end of the *hour*, at least, consisted in "dancing continually ta la ra, ta la ra."

Shall "The Air" ring with the joyous notes of the carols, or breathe low and soft with the sighs of the suffering?

Shall it burst into mad hilarity at the revelry, or wail with the sharp cries of the poor?

It was a painted house, but the paint had worn off; it had a garden, but the garden was choked with weeds; its two rooms were once handsomely furnished, but the furniture was now common and old. It was once a fashionable street; but fashion had fled before the victorious eagles of trade. The tenants of that house were once happy and prosperous. What are they now?

The occupant of the back room was a man, and the occupants of the front room a woman and her children.

He was sitting at a rude deal table; before him were scattered some dirty sheets of music, and around him the place was dreary and bare. By the light of a tallow dip he was playing, in screeching tones, the commonest of ditties and polkas by note. His coat was once of the richest; but now it was old and threadbare. His hands were once white and elegantly shaped; now they were dirty, and blue with cold. His face once beamed with contentment; now it was worn with care and marked by the hard lines of penury.

The other room was darker, and, if possible, more dreary. There were two trundle-beds in a corner, and four bright beings, oblivious to the discomfort, in the happy sleep of childhood. There was a mattress in another corner, with a pile of bedquilts and a sheet.

The fire had burned down to a coal. It shone on the mantle with a sickly glare; and this was the only light there was.

To the mantle-piece were pinned four little stockings, each waiting open-mouthed for a gift from Santa Claus.

Below them crouched a woman, weeping bitterly.

The woman was Clara Hague; and she was weeping because the Christmas dawn would find those little mouths unsatisfied.

Our "Air" is getting mournful,—too mournful for this hour of great joy. The *Te Deum Laudamus*, not the *Miserere*, is for outbursts of gladness like these.

Let it sing of the carriage that surprised the man from his fiddle and the woman from her tears by its thunder in the quiet street.

Let it sing of the warm-hearted brother, forgetting the bitterness of the past, his pockets replenished from a well-saved hoard, who rushed in, startling the little sleepers with his joyous greeting. Let it chant the praises of the hampers of wine, and fowls, and dainties, and the bundles of toys, that same lumbering carriage contained. And last, but not least, let it thrill with the glad shout of a little newsboy, who, frantic with delight, hurried on a new gray suit and a pair of bran-new boots, a present received that very day from his then unknown uncle, John Redfield.

STORY OF A BEAST.

It was a dirty, grasping little office, vile enough to have been built by the Evil One; and the occupant was a dirty, grasping little man, cruel enough to have been made out of its scraps. It was a hard, remorseless little door, that took in a visitor at a gulp and closed after him with a bite. If the luckless caller happened to be a debtor, the fantastic barbarity of his reception was positively infernal. The jerk of grotesque ferocity that greeted him was like the "hoop la!" of a demonized gymnast. The straight-backed chair looked like a part of the stiff, angular man. The yellow-wash on the wall seemed to have caught its reflex from the faded face, and stared grimly at deep lines of avarice ironed into it. Even the mud on the floor, the dust on the table, and the cobwebs on the ceiling maliciously conspired against him, and asserted themselves in every seam of his threadbare clothes. But the face,—stern, stony, relentless, an uncertain compromise between the ghastly severity of a German etching and the constipated austerity of old pictures of the saints,— in that, one fixed idea had blotted out every other vestige of humanity. Each starting vein, bone, and muscle on the hungry visage had "stand and deliver" scarred all over it. The eager metallic glitter of his eyes, the rigid harshness of his mouth, and the nameless craving that seemed to speak from his lean, attenuated cheeks, united to make the name of Hardy Gripstone and Beast synonymous. He looked like a beast, he ate like a beast, he lived like a beast.

Beast started out of every bristle on his unkempt head; it shone in the unhealthy gloss of his battered hat; it wallowed on the stock that clung around his dirty neck; it glistened in the grease on his dingy clothes; it starved on his thin, claw-like hands; it flourished in the grime imbedded under his nails; it creaked in his worn-out, down-trodden shoes. Men, as he shambled by on the streets, unconsciously muttered, "Beast!" women, shrinking from him, whispered, "Beast!" between the heart-throbs the terror of his presence created; children, hushing their cries in silent horror at his grimace, stared "Beast!" out of their wonder-stricken eyes. You might bray him in a mortar and boil the powder in a caldron, yet amid all the envy, hatred, and malice that made up the ingredients, Beast would have triumphantly floated on the top. Beast! Beast! Beast! Beast! The universal verdict clutched him like the shirt of Nessus. He actually grew proud of the title, and received the stigma with a cluck of beastly joy, as though inspired with a certain beastly ambition to deserve it. The laugh with which he hailed any appeal to his charity was monstrous. It commenced with a leathery wheeze like the puff of asthmatic bellows; it croaked with a grating chuckle, as if his throat opened on rusty hinges; and then it broke out in a shrill vocal shudder, that sounded like the shriek of a hyena.

It is an idiosyncrasy of mine to foster just such pet abominations; and I cultivated Hardy Gripstone. My advances were not encouraged by that overweening tenderness that indicates the possible victim of misplaced confidence. Far from "wearing his heart upon his sleeve for daws to peck at," it seemed to have been weaned years agone, and my milk of human kindness fell flat as any whipped syllabub.

Felicitous as were the suggestions of his suspicious brain, it took me fully three months to descend in his bearish estimation from a highwayman to a ninny. There was an incredibility in my apparent lack of motive that puzzled him. His dubious cordiality was doled out under protest. As an exhibitor would clutch a vicious ape, he grabbed at every show of feeling, and almost throttled the most pitiful courtesy, in his nervous dread of its doing him some bodily harm. There was a low cunning in his very acceptance of any little kindness. The sly way in which he insinuated his withered face into my morning papers, and the smirk of satisfaction with which he gloated on the triumph of having gratuitously gleaned their entire contents, was in keeping with every other ludicrous phase of his distorted nature. He looked upon me as a paragon of stupidity; and I fear I considered him a piece of personal property, and felt as much pride in the possession as did Barnum in his Aztec children.

I do not think the acquaintance tended in any way to exaggerate my ideas of human purity. Though it extended through several years, no guilty act I ever heard of detracted from his deserved reputation for beastliness. My surmises never ventured to the hazardous period of infancy, or risked the doubtful thought that kith or kin *could* have loved him; but I have often wondered if there ever *was* a time when his rapacity found employment in the robbing of a hen's nest, or his grasping ambition culminated in the swop of a jack-knife. I wondered if in all the grotesque concomitants that congregated to make up the hideous whole, there existed a redeeming trait. Yes, there was *one*,—one I discovered in the tears that sprung from his unrelenting eyes and rained on his cadaverous cheeks. What was the anguish that shook his beastly frame? what the agony that tore his grasping nature? who was the Moses that smote water from this rock?

Dear hearers, it is here we find the text of the sermon, and here commenceth the preaching.

Early one summer, the grasping little door bit to for good, and I missed its mangy proprietor for probably four months. Had he planted himself in the earth and regerminated, he could not have been more freshened. His emaciated carcass fairly blossomed with magnificence; and gaudy ornament sprouted all over him. It peeped through his shirt-front in flashy studs, it twined on his fingers in glittering rings, it trailed around his waist in glowing velvet, and expanded over his thin legs and arms in a forest of broadcloth. 'Tis true, the shiny collar *would* get over his ears, the coat-sleeves darkened every sparkle on his hands, and the hems of his trowsers persisted in being trodden under heel; but what were petty annoyances like these, in a renovation so complete? His face had been shaved and polished until it approached in glistening amiability the ivory head on a walking-stick; but there was an uncertainty in its ripples of merriment impressive of the belief that if once a genuine ha! ha! was ventured, the galvanized look of joy would instantly vanish. It was at a very uncertain gait he sidled into my office. He did not seem at all sure I would know him, or, in fact, *very* intimately acquainted with himself. The mingled gruffness and cordiality of his greeting suggested a dancing-master suffering with corns. It was a minute or two before his wonted calmness returned; but finally, with a piteous look of blended tenderness and brutal exultation, he handed me a card. It contained the handsomely engraved compliments of Miss Florence Gripstone, and a hope for the pleasure of my company at a soirée. This was the magic wand that turned penury to wealth and made the sterile rock blossom with gorgeous flowers. The beast had a daughter, and with all the ardor of a distorted nature he loved her.

If, a week before, Gripstone's soirée had been hinted, I think I would have laughed; but if the assertion had been ventured that it would be given in a stately house, with spacious grounds, on a fashionable street, and with "Gripstone" on the door-plate, I know I would have shouted outright. Yet the house was stately, and the entertainment superb. Carpets glowing with the gorgeous coloring of the Orient, pictures that had caught their delicate tinge in sacred Rome, furniture carved from the solid heart of rose-wood, plate vying in richness with the state service of a scion of nobility, abounded. Fluttering in the light of many tinted lamps, rare flowers breathed daintiest odors; and floating through the high arches, soft music whispered plaintive ecstasy. In the center of a throng of recently arrived guests, and positively cropping with broadcloth and Marseilles, beamed the host. Close at his side, radiant in her beauty, faultless in its adornment, stood the daughter. In one, a magnificent swallow-tail, fleecy shirt-frill, and snowy gloves had stamped their wearer with a look of hopeless absurdity; in the other, exquisite taste, gentle dignity, and true courtesy bore the impress of glorious womanhood. I was positively bewildered. Could the father of that lovely girl be the wretch the world hooted at? Could the owner of all this grandeur be the Beast I fancied my private property?

Carriage-loads of elegantly attired women crowded each other in the vestibule; dancing beaux congregated in the smoking-room; eminent merchants, with their wives and daughters, wits of both sexes, women of the most exclusive *ton*, thronged the spacious *salons*. Each in their turn was greeted with a smirk of ecstatic glee. To Gripstone the courtesy seemed invested with a proprietary interest. A nod was receipted with a simper, a grasp of the hand with a scrape, the most distant recognition by the most obsequious acknowledgment. There appeared to be no doubt in his mind it was all bought and paid for, but it did no harm to be polite for *once*; and comically polite he was.

I will not say he did not gradually begin to wear the look of a man who had purchased an elephant; for he did. I found him late in the evening posted behind a column and peering through the window at the assembled merry-makers. It was evident he owned the whole party, and that every ringing laugh went with the property; but to him it was a novel investment, and perhaps more difficult to manage than any other article he possessed. Partly from a dim consciousness that he had wandered beyond his depth, and probably from the loneliness consequent to so uncongenial a spectacle, a companion had become necessary; and, when I approached, his jump of cordiality was as uncouth as it was unexpected. So stunned were my senses by the extraordinary events, that, had he cried out, "Come to my arms, my long-lost brother!" or were a strawberry-mark actually found, I could not have been surprised. As it was, his frenzied tugs at the lapel of my coat threatened its immediate destruction, and my spinal column ached under his demoniac slaps on the back, before I gasped out my congratulations.

Wine, excitement, or the society of one who at least had treated him with common decency, warmed the little geniality that remained in him.

With a jerk he thrust me into his study, and, while thrilling music swept through the echoing halls, and the solid flooring swayed under the feet of the dancers, the Beast opened his heart. Shrinking, as though 'twere felony, from the penury of early life, flying from a brief hour of married happiness, in wild triumph he plunged into the dreariness of the upward struggle. Maddened with success, spurning all thought of concealment, with shocking exactness he entered into every detail of the contest, every incident in the appalling history. The low cunning and miserable privation that accumulated the first paltry hundreds, the trickery that made them thousands, the heartless sacrifice of self-respect that doubled and trebled the swelling store, were gloated over with a grin of delight. Transactions imbued with a depravity that made me shudder, were narrated with a chuckle; chicaneries of a depth and maliciousness positively devilish, were touched with a smirk. For *this* he had lied and cheated; for *this* his wretched body grew lean for want of food; for *this* all the world loathed him. In *his* youth poverty *crushed* him; but his little girl, away at school, never knew the meaning of the word. Widows went portionless, but *she* did not want; orphans starved, *her* platter was always full. *He* had been spattered by the coaches of the rich; but now his chariot, and *her* chariot, would take a drive. They had called him Beast; but *now* they called him *gentleman*.

The hundreds who drank his wine and trifled with his sweets called him gentleman, and hundreds more were ready to go down on their knees to his own flesh and blood. Now was the time to enjoy, now the day of happiness. Money was a drug; in his abundance, he could never want. He had love, grandeur, troops of friends; *now* he would live a monarch. Flushed with victory, his eyes blazed, his voice rang clear and loud in its exultation, and his lank form swelled with defiance. Springing to his feet, and clutching up a decanter, he waved it wildly around his head, and, challenging God or man to mar such peace, shivered it on the floor.

Wonder-stricken at the intensity of his vulgarity, and shocked at the sacrilege, I left; and from that moment Hardy Gripstone became a study. Every step in his tortuous course, every phase of his ostentation, every enormity on good taste, was followed with ceaseless vigilance. Excesses that would have startled the most thoughtless were pursued with restless activity; absurdities that drew forth a shout of ridicule were committed with provoking good humor. No freak seemed exuberant, no folly preposterous, no extremity extravagance. The joy of paternity, sinking deep into his nature, made every peculiarity more glaringly apparent. Money had been his idol, its accumulation the summit of his ambition; its reckless sacrifice in his daughter's honor appeared the only adequate expression of his love. The intervals of his devotion were passed in idle boasting, and to me he detailed every incident. There was something really touching in the abject way in which he mentioned each trifle concerning her. Little circumstances connected with her daily life were described as one would describe the traits of some rare animal. His career of degradation seemed to have blunted every idea of responsibility. He looked upon her as a superior being, and her adornment as a sacred duty. The richness of her toilet, the magnificence of her equipage, the glory of her beauty, became an inexhaustible surprise and delight. The utter lack of congeniality, the barrier of caste that divided them, was indescribably sad. Rapturous admiration, gentle amazement, blind idolatry, meek bewilderment, the one twisted by brutality to a living distortion, the other lifted by refinement to the embodiment of womanly grace; and yet they were father and daughter. To do her justice, she strove in every way to testify her love and gratitude for her strange parent; the ties of blood asserted themselves in her words and caresses, but they looked doubtfully out of her eyes. Educated far away from him, and amid other associations, she could not be blind to his faults and shortcomings. The social gulf that divided them, though bridged by her sense of duty, was ever present in her thoughts. I mourned over the remorseless avarice that made him what he was; I almost regretted the culture that placed her so far above him; but, knowing the rude shocks to her sensitive nature, the ruthless trampling on every womanly instinct, I mourned for her the most.

Alas for the schemes of prosy men and women! when tender Loveliness goes airing herself through shady lanes, frank young Valor is seldom far off. The Eurydice may be only a school-girl, and Orpheus a brave, manly boy in a blue coat; but there is a world of heart-fluttering, for all that. The flush of conscious beauty blooming on the cheek of one, is generally a shadow of the warm red that mantles the face of the other. While Eurydice Gripstone mused in quiet nooks, it was no fabled youth of magic lyre who sent the rhetoric and botany waltzing through her brain; and when the fierce cry of "Lights out!" hurried *Jane Eyre* under the pillow, it was no dream of impossible mustaches that made her hear the clocks chime dismally and the cocks crow for midnight.

When the long-looked-forward-to Commencement-day was at length looked *on*, and our heroine tripped up to the platform to read her Essay on Filial Affection, alas for its consistency! it was not the grin of Pluto Gripstone staring stupidly at the show, but the smile of Orpheus, now blessed with a strong beard, that set the recipient of undying fame a trembling. And now, when the farewell had been said, and Orpheus left to break his lyre and mourn,—when Pluto had carried home his prize and the dreary occupation of being as extravagant as possible had commenced,—they were no notes of weird pathos, but billets containing many brave promises, that made strong coffee the most delectable of drinks. Of course all these changes from dreamy reverie to tremulous joy could not escape the searching eye of Pluto; and of course, when questioned, no Eurydice of spirit would think of denying the mate for whom she pined.

Oh, the consternation of the discovery! Oh, the thunders of remonstrance with which Hades resounded! The wheel of Ixion might whirl, and the pitchy depths blaze with the fires of indignation, but all this did not dry the tears of the nymph, nor soothe her bitterness of woe. Every tenderness that could reconcile, every enjoyment that could wean, was vainly essayed; mourning for her Orpheus, she would not be comforted.

At last the Plutonian shadows opened to receive the matchless man. It was with no impossible burst of harmony he charmed away the terrors of this prison-house of injured innocence. Whatever might have been the Orpheus of the fabled "long ago," our modern hero was a plain, business-like man. He thought a great deal of the daughter, but for her worn-out old hulk of a father he didn't care a button. Married he was determined to be, *nolens volens*; and that was the long and the short of it. To a piteous plea to remain and enjoy the old man's wealth, he turned the deafest of ears. Business required his presence at home; where business commanded, he obeyed; and that was the long and the short of that. *He* didn't propose to set up a museum of deformities, if the daughter did; or stay to witness a burlesque on the society he was brought up in, were she never so dutiful.

Oh, the misery of this reality! When shall I forget the anguish on that cadaverous face, when the terror of the narration? For nineteen years he had patiently plodded on, despised by the rich, hated by the poor, spurned by both. He had driven hard bargains that she might drive her carriage; he had turned his wretched debtors houseless into the streets that she might be covered. With every spark of love in his heart, with every instinct of tenderness in his soul, he had bowed down and worshiped her. She had him all: he would set to work anew, were it needful, for her sake; he would go in rags for her; he would starve for her; and this was his reward!—his happiness filched from him by a whipster of a day's acquaintance!

When two people, like the frogs of Æsop, conclude to plunge down a well for the waters of happiness, it is generally the "weaker vessel" who dallies. Let no one suppose our Eurydice quitted the blissful innocence of nymphhood without a struggle, or coolly deserted her battered old father without a regret.

With all the golden halo that hung about the future, there were walks taken in those gardens in which the claw-like hands and tapering fingers clutched each other very tightly, and there were sudden bursts of emotion when the cadaverous cheeks were well-nigh smothered with kisses. If you or I had had an interview with the pillow that adorned her chamber, it would have told us of many a scalding tear that damped its purity and many a smothered sob that fell on its feathery ears. If there were red eyes and pallid cheeks at the breakfast-table on one side, there was a very dismal face on the other. Step by step the hard fact sunk into it, and furrow after furrow marked the progress. It was very glorious for Orpheus; but it was very gloomy for the Beast, and he knew it. Bravely did the old man hold out, and grim and silent was the surrender. Perhaps a dawning light of their ill-assorted association, and a fear for its influence on her happiness, might have opened the sally-port to the conqueror; but he never admitted it. He laid down his arms as coldly and quietly as ever any old Spanish knight gave up his citadel.

Once more the stately house opened wide its doors to a stately gathering, and again there was music and dancing and feasting. There were scores of richly-dressed women to kiss the bride, and there were scores of brave men to congratulate the groom; but there was not one in all that fair company had a kindly word for Hardy Gripstone, and of all the throng who feasted that night there was not one saw his broken heart.

From the hour the creaking steamer bore the happy pair to their Northern home, he slunk out of society. The great house was closed, and the little office, dirtier and more grasping than ever, opened. Every witness to his outburst, myself included, was studiously avoided. I met him often; but no sign of recognition escaped him.

Some months afterward, in passing his filthy little street, I found the remorseless little door had gulped a policeman. Pulling apart its ferocious jaws, and peering in, I saw the straight-backed chair; but the body which seemed a part of it was much stiffer and more angular. The yellow-wash on the wall was a paltry reflex of the ghastly yellow of his faded visage; for the iron face was the face of a corpse.

Men who stood vacantly staring in muttered, "Beast!" women, shrinking from the unsightly spectacle, whispered, "Beast!" and children, gazing in silent horror with the rest, stared "Beast!" out of their wonder-stricken eyes. So hard did they stare, so loud did they mutter, and so many instances did they rehearse of the foul wrongs he had committed, that I am doubtful about the matter myself, and ask you, reader, Was he a Beast?

LEAVES IN THE LIFE OF AN IDLER.

Leaf the First.

When a man whom you have every reason to believe not only the coolest, but the most unimpressible, of beings, suddenly turns white as a ghost and shivers with a nervous spasm, it is safe to suppose he is frightened. But when terror, turning into rage, changes one of the most attentive and respectful of servants into a madman, it is scarcely safe to suppose anything. As it was, I stared in mute amazement, and he glared at me as though I had struck him. While waiting for a light, I carelessly put my hand into a basket of hot-house vegetables. The small egg-plant I took up certainly *did* weigh twenty pounds, and when I attempted to lift the basket the handle bent double; but why this should frighten a man like Marcel, or provoke him to anger, is as inexplicable as it is surprising.

He is pacing up and down the hall in a state of the wildest excitement; and I, with man's truest comfort,—tobacco,—am left to my meditations.

What combination of circumstances reduced him to a porter, I cannot for the life of me imagine. His hand is as soft as a woman's; and his brow has a breadth of brain that would dignify a Senator. Notwithstanding the scrupulous deference in his tone, his manner possesses the quiet ease of a gentleman, to as great a degree as any I ever saw.

The utter incongruity of his appearance and position struck me the moment I laid eyes on him. He flourished his napkin with the dainty grace of a courtier; and when he lifted my luggage to his shoulder, I was on the point of apologizing. He makes my bed, polishes my shoes, performs with fidelity the most menial offices; and yet I *cannot* but look upon him as an equal. Poor devil! His cheek may burn with the bluest blood in France. What a pity the world is not moral!

There is something enchanting to me in smoking. It is like a rich cordial,—nerving every faculty to action. A draught from your *Cabanas*, the pulse quickens, the mind clears, and thought awakes, like a fine instrument under the magic touch of a master. The wind moans drearily without, the rain beats dismally against the windows, the fagots flicker blue-flamed and weird in the dark recesses of the chimney-place; but what care I? The white walls are lurid in the flare, the great bed stands out in the darkness like a grotesque engine of the Inquisition; but who suffers? *Au troisième, No. 30, Rue Lepelletier*, was never noted for its comforts; but who would ask a repose more secure, a peace more perfect, than are enjoyed by the occupant of this rambling old house? Blessed be the earth that bears this solace for weary brains! Its very odor is pregnant with dreams of the *Vuelta Abajo*. You see the luxuriant foliage of the tropics, the dark-green waves curling on the coral beach, and the scarlet flamingoes that gather shell-fish in the marshes away off in the golden sunset. You hear the wild song of the Spanish fruit-man as he sculls his boat along the broken wharves, and are soothed into utter listlessness by the thousand perfumes that come off with the land-breeze. A taste of the fragrant vapor, you recline in the odorous orange darkness of a dream-land, languidly breathing the smoke from your hookah, and the lustrous leaves moving over you are bathed in the soft and melting sunshine. The day lingers luminously over far mountain-ranges, paling in brilliancy on the hill-side, where the blushing vine, bending with the clusters, is still enlivened by the song of the vintagers; and in the valley, where the grain sheds its gold under the sickle. You are lost in voluptuous reverie. You breathe the sunlight; intellect is thawed and mellowed; emotions take the place of thought; "your senses, sun-tranced, rise into the sphere of soul." You feel the heart of humanity throbbing through all nature, and your own warms into quivering life.

"It is not good for man to live alone;" and you dream of another to share the rapture your wild fancy has created.

Your Haidee is pure. Her form has rather the statuesque roundness of Psyche than the luxurious excess of Venus. Timid, yet not tremulous, graceful even to delicacy, coquettish in outline, *her* beauty is formed for smiles. She is a still-eyed Xenobi, but knows nothing of Passion with disheveled locks, divine frenzy, and fiery grasp. She is your friend and comforter; and you are the strong rock her helplessness clings to. Your uncouth manner softens as you behold her troubled look. You become kind and considerate. You watch with pity the pinched faces of anxiety that pass before you. You cheer the little beggar, and give him of your abundance. Unhappy wanderer! he has started early on his wretched pilgrimage for bread. "Your heart, enlarged by its new sympathy with one, grows bountiful to all." The fragrant smoke curls in heavier clouds, and is wafted imperceptibly into the darkness. Ah, Arthur Granger! Arthur Granger! you are dreaming impossibilities, as the man athirst dreams of flowing waters.

"Love has lost its wings of heavenly azure with which it soared light as a lark into the empyrean, and now grovels on the earth, weighed down by the burden of red gold."

How well I recollect that warm, balmy March morning! My mother had sent me to Paris about six months before, to read law with an old relative. Of course I was delighted; but that day I felt tired of the dull routine of my life, and longed for the green fields, waving trees, and wild mountain-torrents of my home. I was walking slowly down the street, thinking gloomily of the labors of another day, and she was standing near a school-house door, intently occupied in giving some directions to an old soldier. In my whole life I do not think I ever saw a more beautiful creature. The airiness of the lithe little figure, the playfulness in the nod of the graceful head, the look of joyous innocence on that perfect face, flitted through my mind like a bright ray of sunshine during the entire day. Every morning, for years after, I met that child; and every morning her beaming smile cheered my young life like a glimpse of heaven. I never spoke to her; it was a long time before she even knew of my existence; but by-and-by I noticed a quizzical expression come over the old man's face, and I saw her features warm with a faint flush of recognition. How many dreams I based on that slight fabric! Of course I discovered her name; and of course I learned that her father was very rich; but what was that to me? With what pride did I gaze at his name in huge gilt letters on a great warehouse near us, and what wonderful little gothic cottages did I build on the strength of the "and Son" that would shortly be added to it! The long nights with my cousin became less wearisome. I could hear the dull creaking of the letter-press, and see him sit poring over his writing, quite patiently. When the organ-grinder stopped on the corner and played "Make me no gaudy chaplet," I did not long to rush into the streets, for I had *her* to think about. When the clock struck eleven, and my cousin, with his peculiar "phew!" commenced another letter, I looked on quite calmly, and began the construction of another cottage. Of course there were rainy days, and Thursdays that were ages to me; and there were Christmas holidays, and long, hot vacations, that she did not come; but September brought back the radiant face, and I worshiped on.

Gradually I noticed a change in her dress. She wore little lace collars, and bright ribbons I had not seen before; and sometimes she carried a little bouquet of violets, with a white rosebud in the center. As she grew older, I had many rivals. Gallant youths, brave in broadcloth and beavers, followed by dozens the *Picciola* I had watched so tenderly. How proudly I passed them by! and how I sneered at the thought of their understanding *her*!

I saw her form grow fuller and expand into a more queenly beauty. I saw her eyes sparkle with a diviner light, and her bosom swell with new and strange emotions. I watched her until she became a woman, and gloried in her matchless loveliness.

At last the end came. One morning, the brown calico frock was changed for an India silk, and the little school bonnet, with its blue veil, for a new one, covered with artificials. She was accompanied by an elderly lady, and looked nervous and excited. I was troubled at the tremulous, uncertain expression of her face. The next day I read her name in the list of graduates.

It does generally rain at picnics; but this time it didn't. When shall I ever forget that picnic? I stole a holiday to attend it. It was late when I arrived: the dinner was over, and I had one prepared expressly for me. Would you believe it? my fair attendant was the little Blue Veil. She was so kind and so gentle, and treated me in such a confiding, sisterly way. There was a tenderness in the soft depths of her eyes, a purity in the dazzling loveliness of her face, that my heart yielded to with the blind fervor of a devotee. When shall I ever forget that evening walk under the trees? Oh! those buttercups and daisies, and little Quaker ladies! what recollections they bring back to me! The pressure of that soft little hand on my arm, the timid grace of her manner, the sound of her clear, girlish voice, with what emotions have they stirred my soul! Heaven bless her! Thank God for that one glorious picture! It was years ago; she is married now, and the mother of children; yet even now I sometimes catch myself standing on the corners and gazing wistfully down the street for the bright image that stole into the morning of my young life like a soothing dream in a long, troubled sleep.

Leaf the Second.

Gardening in midwinter!—what new freak has taken possession of that eccentric man? The morning broke dank and drear, for the December air had chilled the moisture into a fog. The wide verandas that opened on the court-yard in rear were dripping with the rain, and the broad flag-stones covered with a greasy slime. The diminutive grass-plot was brown and soggy, but the withered blades rapidly disappeared under the sturdy plunges of Marcel's spade. I had gone out on the gallery to fill a ewer with water—in his excitement of the previous evening, Marcel had forgotten my morning bath—and saw him distinctly through the *jalousies*. He must have commenced at daylight; for, though it was then early, the ground was almost entirely dug up. Near him, on the pavement, was the basket over which he had displayed so much agitation. He prepared six holes, each of which was carefully lined with straw, and then deliberately commenced planting the egg-plants *whole*.

An hour or two later, he came up with the coffee. I thought he turned a shade or two paler at seeing me up and dressed; but no vestige of petulance remained. Having really taken no offense at the outburst, I rallied him concerning it.

"I was wrong," said he, gravely; "but nature has left me destitute of tact. An artist was once ordered to paint a one-eyed princess: the artful man made the picture a profile. Devoid of his discernment, I saw only my ruined treasures."

"And, after acting like a wild man, you sneer at my curiosity."

"One so secure in his position as M. Granger can lose nothing by forbearance."

"In other words, I am to endure patiently the taunts of an apron, because its wearer is worthy of a surtout?"

"The prompt nature of hunger is well known. Fifty years ago, I might have shrieked in the *Place de la Concorde.* France has degenerated; I polish your shoes."

The assumption of inferiority was so defiant that I said, bluntly, "This can never excuse the neglect of faculties bestowed by Heaven."

He shrugged his shoulders, and answered, "There was a time when power succumbed to intellect. 'Stand out of my sunlight,' said Diogenes to Alexander; and Alexander did so. This is Paris, M. Granger, and we are living on the *Rue Lepelletier.*"

"And, frightened at its splendor, M. Marcel has prudently determined to put his brains under regimen."

"M. Marcel has prudently determined to avoid in future a *tête-à-tête* with his superiors."

He started abruptly to the door, and I called him back; determined distance even in a servant is far from flattering, and I asked him frankly if his visits to my apartments were as distasteful as his manner would lead me to infer.

He answered, politely, "Were fickle Fortune waiting to conduct me to the summit of my ambition, I would detain her a few hours to enjoy society so charming; but M. Granger forgets he is addressing a domestic."

"Stubborn in your pride to the last! What am I to think of one who holds all sympathy in contempt?"

"*Basta!*" he fiercely exclaimed. "I am like a vagrant cur: flying from the sticks and stones of a vile rabble, I fawn with cringing servility on the first hand that throws me a crust."

"Wrong, Marcel; wrong," I earnestly answered. "You are trying to warp your nature, as you tried to force the fruits of summer to bloom and ripen in midwinter. You *will* be human, and your egg-plants will rot in the earth."

My words seemed to have taken away every particle of color there was in him. His eyes contracted until they resembled those of a wild animal, and for a moment I thought he was going to spring at my throat. His voice—when finally he regained it—sounded like that of another person.

"M. Granger," said he, "a man visiting the *Jardin des Plantes* once undertook to stroke a leopard. Strange as it may appear, the animal was more pleased with petting than the inquiring mind imagined. The instant our naturalist attempted to desist, the creature raised his paw to strike. There monsieur stood, for a whole night, gazing into his glaring eyes and smoothing his soft neck. Can you imagine his feelings?"

With a bow that would have graced the Duc de Beaumont, he left. I heard him hastily packing his modest wardrobe; and in fifteen minutes a tilbury had whirled him away—whither, Heaven only knows.

Leaf the Third.

I do not think his own mother would call him handsome; he is certainly not young, nor particularly brilliant; and yet there is a fascination about the proprietor of this rambling old house that gave me an unaccountable desire to become his tenant. He is a wine-merchant, and occupies, as his counting-room, the entire second floor. The place is desolate-looking and dusty, and the furniture old with service; but, I am told, no man in Paris controls more of the grand vintages than M. Pontalba. With a Frenchman, the *legality* of a transaction depends on its being negotiated in a *café*; and it was in one of these I first saw him. He was seated at a table near me, absorbed with the contents of a box of baby-clothes, while a rather pretty and exceedingly voluble *modiste* harangued him on their beauty. The tenderness of his expression struck me. He took out the articles one by one, examining each with the interest of a woman. He ran his fingers through the tiny sleeves, and smoothed out the ruffles and lace, with a care that was almost loving. Diminutive cambric shirts, snowy dresses, and silky flannels,—all in their turn were inspected and replaced with a sigh of satisfaction.

An ardent young friend and I had been discussing the merits of Comte's philosophy; but so attracted were we by the singular trait that both stopped involuntarily, and watched him, until the woman was paid and a messenger carried the fairy wardrobe away.

My friend was an enthusiastic metaphysician; and, resuming the subject with a zest, was soon plunged into the phenomena of thought, the action of the brain, and the vitality of the blood that sustained it. As all conversant with the subject can readily believe, not many minutes elapsed before his artful sophistries proved the non-existence of heaven, hell, and even God himself.

M. Pontalba turned suddenly, and, drawing his chair close beside us, with an apology for the seeming intrusion, addressed the incipient skeptic:

"Behind the iron bars of that dreariest of studies, a prison, a little weed once received the concentrated thought of a savant. The covering of its stem, the first tender leaves, the development of the bud, the expansion of the flower—each bewildering in its consummate propriety—unfolded, in their turn, a system of laws in simplicity transcendent. By the aid of a microscope, a 'gillyflower' was seen protecting a chrysalis. Warm leaves cherished it, dainty juices aided its digestion, wholesome offshoots nourished it to maturity. Eking out a scant existence between two granite flags, this insignificant waif reared a caterpillar. What man are you, who can say there is no God?"

There was a pathos in his voice, and a tone of simple fervor, which gave that quiet old man the air of a priest.

It was more than a year afterward I took these rooms; but my establishment was of short duration ere I learned the history of an eventful morning which followed that incident:—of how the placid face of the master peered among his people, beaming with a great joy; how a sumptuous feast was fitted up in the private office for all in the employ; of the two hundred francs, and a suit of clothes, presented to each; and how every one, from the little messenger to the gray cashier, with the rarest wine in the cellar, drank prosperity to the new-born son and heir, and much happiness to the mother,—"God bless her!"

Once I saw a pony-carriage, with an aged, semi-military driver, pull up at the door, and the flutter of a veil as the vehicle passed through the entrance; and this was the only glimpse I ever caught of the little lady that dingy office called mistress. There was, however, a certain briskness in the movement of the clerks, and a glow of pleasure on their faces, that always denoted a visit; and very frequent those visits were. Without in any way obstructing it, her pretty interest seemed to throw a halo around the dull routine of trade; and, if there was any unpleasantness, the arrival of Jean Palliot, coachman and ex-grenadier, with Madame Althie Pontalba, was sure to drive it away.

Why *will* my heart, like a hungry thing, gloat on the happiness of others? He has gone away—in the midst of the holidays—no one knows whither; and his sweet wife and pleasant home are as dreary as I. There is a mystery about this house which I have not yet unraveled. Marcel left in the morning, and M. Pontalba in the evening. That has been two weeks ago. I thought he would have fainted when I told him of the *garçon's* exodus. I attempted a history of the gardening; but he would not listen to a word, and remained locked up in his private room during the entire day. Late in the evening a stranger called, and insisted on an interview. It resulted in a hasty consultation with the cashier, and an order for a coach. The two went off together,—whither, or for how long, no one knows.

Leaf the Fourth.

To-day finds a man in the full glow of health, and strength, and happiness; to-morrow comes death, cold, pitiless, irresistible; mocking all hope, freezing desire, crushing all effort with the eternal law of time and human destiny, it strikes him down with the icy fury of a fiend. Poetry, passion, humanity, are shivered at the touch. The glorious creature who, an instant before, quivered with life and love and energy, lies a shapeless mass, disgusting to the sight, loathsome to the touch, revolting to every instinct of our nature. So, in its ceaseless routine, forever and forever, wheels on the world. The play-ground bully, the swindler of the corn exchange, who is the more virtuous? dolls with life, babies with genius, which the more sensible? Even baby has its "pat-a-cake, pat-a-cake," and is lulled to sleep with visions of a coach and six little ponies. Dreams, dreams of self, that man wraps himself in like the swathing of a mummy. Who ever saw a cake marked with "T," who ever a "Valley of Tranquil Delight"?

The sun rises and sets on the weary diamond-digger of the South, the crazed perfume-hunter in the East, the stifled hemp-curer in the fetid swamps of Russia, the shriveled iron-worker in the scorching furnaces of England. Here, in Paris, amid that motley herd who feed on virtue, the moon shines down calmly on purblind embroiderers and peerless beauties, on worn-out *roués* and squalid beggars. The breeze that wafts to heaven the pure prayer of the maiden witnesses the fierce ribaldry of the courtesan; it flutters the curls of a sleeping infant, and bears on its wings the whispered exchange of *chastity for bread*. And man goes on, devouring his three poor meals a day, and babbling the meaningless nothings he has learned by rote. Oh, land of enlightenment! Oh, age of Christianity! Oh, zenith of civilization!

The smoke-wreaths curl into thicker clouds. I have painted bright pictures, and they have faded. I have cherished fond dreams, and they are vanished. "It is not good for man to live alone;" and I am most solitary. I can make another picture,—without the roses; but it will be true.

It's a merry Christmas, this Twenty-fifth of December, eighteen hundred and eighty-seven,—a very merry Christmas; times have scarcely changed at all in the last thirty years. The sun shines down brightly, and the frosty air is fall of gladness; for Santa Claus, with his untold wonders, has come and gone. Ecstasies over dolls and transports over tea-sets, screams of delight at hobby-horses and enthusiastic exclamations at humming-tops, have passed. Paint-boxes and writing-desks, leaden soldiers and tin trumpets, at last, are reduced to blissful matters of course. The streets, which all the morning have been thronged with laughing groups of happy children, are now almost deserted. Senators and cabmen, ministers of state and town constables, romping school-girls and worn-out actresses, *Lady Dedlock* and her washer-woman, men, women, and children of all degrees, have quietly seated themselves to roasted turkey and plum-pudding. Even the little boys who *will* play marbles under the library windows, who are constantly being "fat" and wanting "ups" and "roundings," and who are invariably ordered to "knuckle down and bore it hard," are now intently occupied with the succulent delights of "drum-sticks" and gizzards. And yet the man whose fingers now form these letters *then* sits alone. Time has not passed lightly over *his* head. The few hairs that straggle from beneath his skull-cap are gray, and the faintest breath makes him wrap closer in his thickly-wadded dressing-gown. His face is worn and pale, and the wrinkled hand, though it only holds a little cigarette, will sometimes tremble as it moves. The Christmas dinner is pushed away untasted. *Château-Margaux* has lost its flavor, and silver and crystal do not bring appetite now. Even the glowing sunshine, which plate-glass and silk damask cannot keep out, is unheeded. He gazes wearily at the magnificent furniture, and smokes. He has talked much to the world, and it has heard him. Flung into life without a friend, governed only by the will of a race born to command, he has struggled through sneers and sarcasm to eminence. Men fear him now, women flatter, nearly all envy; yet he is alone. He knows this; he knows that in all the laughing groups who enjoy this wine-drinking and turkey-eating day his name has not been mentioned once. Nature allows no trifling with her laws; flowers do not bloom in deserts. He has crushed sentiment; he has stifled affection. With a heart by nature kindly, he sits now an image cut in steel. He gazes calmly at his desolate hearth, at his joyless age, and smokes. Man has no power to move him; fate condemned him to be a statue.

Ah! the strongest, after all, are but weak, erring, human beings. The last of a race stands weary and old, trembling on the brink of eternity. Who will close the fading eye? Who will smooth the dying pillow? With all his great wealth, with all his wondrous knowledge, what one deed of charity will that infirm old man take into the presence of his Creator? He looks dreamingly out at the window. The plate-glass and damask are not there now; the sunshine is warm and the air balmy. A mild, breezy March morning, and he is standing on a corner, looking far down the street. "She is coming, coming;" the dark eyes beam on him, and the radiant face flushes the pallor of his cheek;—"come." He gives one lingering, beseeching look at the passing figure, the cigarette drops to the carpet, the withered hands clasp convulsively the arms of the chair, the gray head slowly falls on his breast, and one more frail human being, exhausted with the anxieties of a long and bitter life, is at rest forever. It's a merry Christmas, this Twenty-fifth of December, eighteen hundred and eighty-seven,—a very merry Christmas. Times have scarcely changed at all in the last thirty years.

How he ever got there, or when, I do not now, nor will I ever, know, but when I looked up Marcel was standing before me.

"M. Granger," said he, abruptly, "it will be necessary for you to seek another lodging."

"Why?"

"I would do you a service. The proof lies in the future. This house is doomed."

"Poor Marcel," said I, with genuine pity, "some recent trouble has turned your brain!"

"Mad!" he replied, laughing bitterly. "The wonder is that I am not. For years I have been hunted,—hunted like a dog. Prisons have been my dwelling-place, disguises my only clothing. My pillow is a spy; the very atmosphere I breathe is analyzed."

"And what is your offense?"

"A desire to live as the great God intended an Italian should. A desire to lift to his place among the free-born the corrupt descendant of Coriolanus, now nourishing his miserable body on the *scudi* extorted from a stranger's patience. The vile crew whom our ancestors drove howling and naked across the Danube, in undisturbed apathy gloat over our dearest treasures. Our people are ground into the dust; our women, stripped in the market-place, shriek under the pitiless lash of the oppressor. One man, sworn to protect Italy with his life, can save her, and has refused. That man dies."

"And you are pledged to kill him?"

"I am pledged to see you safely without these walls by this day fortnight."

"And you?"

"I remain."

"Marcel, you are crazy."

"M. Granger, you are polite."

That night fortnight I was away; and this was the message that sent me:

> "TO M. ARTHUR GRANGER:
>
> "Your fatal discovery on the morning of my departure makes you the only man to whom I can appeal. Let me pray the appeal be not in vain. In the folly of my youth, while sojourning in Italy, I joined a powerful secret order, whose demands cease only with death, and whose penalty for denial is a sudden and bloody end. You can judge, then, my anxiety on being compelled to admit to my establishment, disguised as a servant, one of its highest officers, and my horror at hearing of his abrupt departure. Since then I have learned the unhappy cause. My life is in another's hands. It is for him to command, and for me blindly to obey. There are two beings in this world dearer to me than my soul's salvation. To you, M. Granger, as a Christian gentleman, I commend them. The sealed note inclosed (the contents of which are a matter of life and death) I beg you will at once deliver to my wife; and let me conjure you, until the crisis is over, to make my house at Romainville your home.

"ÉDOUARD PONTALBA."

Leaf the Last.

This is the 15th of January, 1858. France is in a blaze of excitement. Last evening, in the *Rue Lepelletier*, an attempt was made to assassinate the Emperor, by throwing grenades filled with fulminating mercury under the coach that bore the Imperial family to the Italian Opera. Count Felice Orsini, the murderer, himself desperately wounded, has been arrested, and Paris is crying for his blood.

For several days I have been the honored guest of Madame Althie Pontalba. It is a golden evening; the sky, an hour ago so clear and blue, is piled with golden clouds, and stretches out into golden rivers, with golden banks, flowing calmly down into a golden sea. The purple slates on the church-steeple, the red tiles on the house-tops, the gardens with their evergreens and jonquils and little blue violets shrinking out of the frosty air, are wrapped in a golden mist. The light streams through the windows in rays of pure gold, and trickles down the walls in little golden currents. It is an enchanting little villa. The steep gables covered with variegated slate, the thin fluted columns of the verandas, the diminutive marble steps, the broad bow-windows with their transparent plate-glass, look more like a fairy picture than a reality. The trim shrubbery, the airy little statues, and even the white palings, so frail and fanciful in their construction, are charmingly appropriate.

It is an enchanting little room. The icy air is warmed by the bright carpet and glowing curtains, and the trickling currents of golden light on the walls are mellowed by the blazing sea-coals. It is a merry little fire, an ardent, earnest, *home* fire, that shoots out its whimsical little flames as if it meant to burn one to a cinder, and flutters and murmurs to itself and scatters down the white feathery ashes in a very ecstasy of impetuous glee. The green porcelain tiles on the hearth, the oval-shaped chairs, the wonderful tables, and the little easy-chair, are all flushed up, and seem quite enlivened at its sportive tricks. The silver sewing-bird, with its glittering little garnet eyes, is peering curiously down at the painted fish-geranium on the teapot; and the geranium, sweltering by the fire, seems almost wilted with the heat. The teapot pants and struggles under its steaming contents, and looks appealingly at the great china cup on the table; and now a lump of sparkling sugar is dropped into its shiny recesses, and the fragrant odor of that gentlest soother of troubled thoughts pervades the room.

How shall I describe the mistress of this fairy resting-place, as she sits in the softened light of this golden winter evening, with the trickling golden currents and the quivering firelight playing on her dress, and the last rays of the sunshine melting into golden threads in her hair? How can I picture the look of girlish innocence on her face, the artless grace of her manner, her delicate feminine ways, and the dainty arrangement of her toilet? How can I tell of the irresistible charm that pervades every article about her, from the little French boot resting on the rug, to the ruffle that circles her white throat? The balmy morning of her young life has passed. The brown calico frock, and the little school bonnet, with its blue veil, have been put away forever. The lithe figure has grown matronly, the childish timidity is gone; the softened face tells of changes,—changes made by much happiness; changes also, alas! by trouble.

The dark eyes beam with a deeper tenderness, with a wealth of maternal devotion, with a world of maternal anxiety. The aurora, with its hazy glow, has disappeared, and now the sun shines brightly on the early day; yet through all the love, and all the care, and all the joy of her pure life, remains that radiant smile, the glorious creation of a glorious God, that awakens in man one sensation,—tranquillity. O man, with the joy of your *own* young love, O woman blessed with a remembrance of earlier days, is it needful I should say, Madame Althie Pontalba is the Little Blue Veil?

There were two visitors here an hour ago,—a lady and a gentleman. Whatever their lack of ostentation, there was an air of distinction about both that would strike the most casual observer.

The cabriolet was plain, but the horses showed the purest blood, and the harness and equipments a neatness one would not see in a day's ride. The gentleman was tall and stately, with a well-shaped aquiline nose, and a mustache and imperial pointed *à la militaire*; and the lady was petite and graceful, with a face of rare loveliness. The features of both told plainly of a great trial bravely endured. The lady entered alone. Her carriage and demeanor possessed all that quiet elegance which is only met with in the society of the great; but it was with no courtly speech she addressed the mistress of this quiet home. To twine her arms lovingly around that dear form, to draw it close to her bosom, to pour out, in a voice broken with tears, a burst of gratitude, was the mission. In moments when hearts are wrung, we do not practice our grand politeness. A noble life had been saved, a terrible calamity averted. The polished manner of the *salon* was dropped. A *wife* spoke, a *woman* listened. The visit was already a long one when Jean Palliot took charge of the equipage, and, on leaving, it was into *his* hand the gentleman thrust a roulette of Napoleons.

"Sir," cried the indignant coachman, "a soldier of the Grand Army is not a beggar."

"It is not the gold, but the portraits of his commander I give the soldier of the Grand Army."

"*Mon Dieu!*" exclaimed the now affrighted veteran, "it is Napoleon!—*Vive l'Empereur!*"

Of the history of that attempt on the life of Napoleon, the world is fully informed. That, thanks to a fortunate warning, the Imperial coach was lined with boiler-iron, is well known. That warning, by direction of her husband, was written by Madame Althie Pontalba, and delivered by me.

That the destructive missiles were manufactured in Birmingham, England, our Minister Plenipotentiary has good cause to remember; but that they were smuggled into Paris in the guise of egg-plants, and deposited in the grass-plot in rear of house No. 30 of that now memorable street, I believe is still a mystery.

That Count Felice Orsini (the man executed) was concealed for weeks, is on record at the Prefecture; but that he assumed the position of a servant, and the name of Marcel, is not.

As for me, I think a great deal, and say nothing; but if the young Pontalba, who now studies type-setting with the Prince Imperial, was not the baby whose clothes I once saw examined at a *café* there is no truth in these "Leaves of an Idler."

MR. BUTTERBY RECORDS HIS CASE. [A]

J. Moses Butterby, aged 40 years; a licensed broker; nativity, American; temperament, sanguine; habit, slightly obese; constitution, robust. History of the case as related by himself.

I don't see how I ever came to *be* married. It was certainly the last thing my friends expected of me, and it was the last thing I ever expected of myself; but that I am married, Mrs. J. Moses Butterby, and Master Alphonso Moses Butterby, are both here to testify.

What so aristocratic a family found in me to admire is as much a secret now as then. I don't think it was intellect; for I am afraid that when Nature designed me the "shining" element was left out. Somehow, at school, the composition sent to the village journal was never mine; the declamation repeated at every fresh arrival of directors was always another's; and if, by any chance, a visitor asked to hear a recitation, under no circumstances was I ever invited to show off. My modest part in society was not crowned with greater success. Ma (dear heart!) objected to dancing, and I never learned; I didn't go to picnics, for I don't know how to drive; I tried smoking, and it made me sick; if I drank wine, I was sure to go to sleep: in fact, none of the amusements of other young men ever amused me; and the result was, the money they spent, I saved.

Envious people have hinted at this as the attraction which first caught the respected mother of my Malinda Jane and the respected mother-in-law of myself; but ideas so unbecoming I repel with proper scorn.

I do not think myself more stupid than the average of mankind; but, somehow, while they walked through the middle of the streets, I sought the narrow alleys; and while others aspired to noise and distinction, I found retirement and Malinda Jane. (It *was* in an alley I first met Mrs. J. Moses Butterby—though this in no way concerns the present narrative.)

Malinda Jane (I trust I am not violating any matrimonial law in thus familiarly speaking of my respected helpmeet)—Malinda Jane, from the first time I beheld her, up to the present period of a long, and I may say intimate, acquaintance, appears to me a paragon of all the modest and retiring virtues. If among her many attractions she is possessed of a distinguishing trait, it lies in the power of her eyes. So much language do their depths contain, that to me, at least, any other is in a great measure a superfluity. I should be afraid to count up the consecutive hours we have spent in this silent converse, reading each other's hearts, as some pleasant poet has styled it, "through the windows of the soul." I would not have you suppose them almond-shaped or piercing. No! Malinda Jane's eyes are round. It was their gentle blue that enchanted me; and there I found the congeniality that cheered my drooping spirit.

Looking back now upon our courtship, I am inclined to think it must have been uninteresting to a third party; but there is no denying the fact that to us it was most soothing, and well calculated to develop our mutual affection.

I have no accurate recollection of the event vulgarly called "popping." Fortunately, I congratulate myself on escaping that breach of decorum. If you join my friends in asking "how it came about," I reply, "Naturally." The morning Malinda Jane's mother asked me if I had decided upon October the 24th or November the 24th, I unhesitatingly answered, "November the 24th, if you please;" and the whole affair was accomplished.

I have said before, Malinda Jane is not of a demonstrative disposition, but thinks (if I may strain a point) ponderously. I have never known her to manifest any will in opposition to my own; and, since I come to think of it, I do not remember her ever manifesting a will in opposition to any one else. In this general term I of course include Master Moses Alphonso Butterby and my most highly respected mother-in-law. Such a family, according to all rule precedent, should be superlatively happy; but there seems to be a disturbing element in all families, and mine, alas! proved no exception. It came about thus.

Among the few parting words of my deceased ma were, "Mosie" (she always called me Mosie), "never live with your mother-in-law." Treasuring the command, as I may say I treasured everything the dear old lady left, including the property, when finally the day *was* fixed, I set about obeying it. On an occasion when Mrs. Mountchessington Lawk—the name of my respected mother-in-law—had described our imaginary bower, and her imaginary apartment adjoining, until she had worked herself into a fever of imaginary happiness, I mildly communicated the behest of my departed parent.

The scene which followed I can only characterize as indescribably touching. The look of blank despair on the face of Malinda Jane, and the tears of rage and mortification that suffused the aristocratic nose of her ma, I frankly confess, went to the bottom of my heart. It was many months before I ceased to regret this rude banishment of their hopes; but, looking upon it from my present stand-point, I am compelled to admit my dear dead ma was right.

The only accident worthy of remark that happened to Malinda Jane on our wedding-day was a fright. I have reason to congratulate myself at its occurring *on* that day, instead of a few weeks subsequent. The consequences in the latter event, it is needless to say to married people, might have been serious.

Passing out of the church-door, we were confronted by a drunken cobbler, who, in a wild and insane manner, proposed "three cheers for Jinny." The assembled crowd of dilapidated urchins hanging around the steps proceeded to give them with a vim faintly suggestive of ridicule. The single glance I obtained of the discourteous offender gave me an idea of chimneys. His face was smoky, his clothes were fleecy, and his general appearance was decidedly sooty throughout. A shock head, and more shocky eyebrows, bore a strange resemblance to the patent chimney-sweep; while his clothes seemed rich in past memories of the profession. I had before caught sight of this individual, in a tumble-down, rickety shop near the residence of Mrs. Mountchessington Lawk. I had, in fact, seen her on more than one occasion bestowing charity upon him in the form of broken victuals; but the recollection failed entirely to account for the effect of his cheers for "Jinny" upon the too tender nerves of my dear wife and her distinguished mother. I attributed the emotion to the trying nature of the ceremony we had just passed through. Reflecting that people do not get married every day, and appalled at the terrible conclusions with which the mind would distract itself by pondering so alarming a topic, I shudderingly abandoned it, and assisted Malinda Jane and her ma, in a fainting condition, to the carriage.

It is needless to say that the cobbler was at once given in charge to a policeman. The next morning, in consideration of a handsome fee, he moved away. I accomplished this out of regard to the feelings of Mrs. Lawk; but, I must confess, I never regretted anything more.

The commencement of married life (as many married men will bear me out) is even more consoling than the happiest days of courtship. The smell of varnish on new furniture is as delightfully novel as the odor of the orange-blossoms; the brightness of the new carpets and the crispness of the new curtains both mark an era,—even if the stove *is* obstinate about drawing or a man *is* called out of bed to put up the coffee-mill. There was Malinda Jane's night-robe hanging on one side of the bed, and there was my night-robe on the other. My clothes were in the upper drawer of the bureau, hers were in the lower—in such delightful and loving proximity that I own to feeling a new man; I gloried in having some one dependent on me: in short, I was happy.

I will not deny that there was some trouble about servants (I think Malinda Jane had seven the first ten days). True, the meals were not models of regularity; the chicken sometimes came on in too natural a state,—blue and pulpy,—and the beefsteak betrayed a volcanic appearance, as though reduced to lava by an irruption of gravy. I remember one woman stole a keg of butter, and another went off with half a dozen silver spoons. The former, Malinda Jane ascribed to the cat; the latter, to a defective memory; but, then, Malinda

Jane never learned housekeeping (I don't see why she should, poor dear!), and trifles like these failed to mar *our* household peace.

I would mention the conduct of Mrs. Mountchessington Lawk as being, for nearly a year, really saintly. Even the rare intervals at which she visited were marked by a manner the reverse of familiar. Almost every evening she would stand on the opposite side of the street, gazing wistfully at us as we sat in the window; but no persuasion induced her to pay a formal visit more than once a fortnight.

With this striking evidence of my wisdom before me, I grew worldly. I think that during that short year I possessed a better opinion of myself and my capacity than ever before or since.

Worse than this, I grew pharisaical. I ventured to pity my less fortunate neighbors, bound hand and foot to the slavery of mothers-in-law. I attempted to joke them, and poke them severely in the ribs with my knuckles, when the magic name was mentioned. So often did I congratulate myself on the shrewd stroke of genius displayed, that I fear even her respectability became sadly impaired in my mind, and depreciated to such an extent that I was gradually led to think of her irreverently as an "old gal."

"Too much for you, old gal," got to be an exclamation so wonderfully consoling that, it crept into my sleep, and in those halcyon days I often waked up by the side of Malinda Jane, muttering the words, "Too much for you, old gal." Waked up, I think I said. Ah! would I had never waked up, particularly on the dismal clouds which for a season darkened my domestic sunshine!

Scarce half a twelvemonth elapsed, ere the retiring disposition of Malinda Jane seemed to shrink into even greater seclusion. I frequently found her powerful mind wandering, and her eyes fixed on vacancy. In our evening walks, which invariably preceded retiring for the night, she leaned heavily on my arm.

Although the appearance of our daily repasts did not seem to justify it, the cash demands for market-bills suddenly became enormous; and, when I expostulated, my reasonable objections only produced tears. An apparently needless grief had crept into our quiet home, and a lack of confidence that pained me. For many weeks I helplessly pondered the unaccountable mystery.

At last (oh that it had taken any shape but that!) the enigma developed itself. Returning home one day, I had straightened my collar and smoothed my hair before opening the door (feeling a proper pride in my personal appearance, these preparations are usually a preliminary step), when suddenly, just as the portal moved on its hinges, my sense of smell was saluted with the odorous fumes of gin. From the first suffocating whiff of this aromatic cordial do I date the commencement of my grief. Malinda Jane, I knew, never indulged in as much as a sip of Cologne: so, convinced that the breach of discipline was the guilty act of a servant, with all the offended dignity I could embody in my deportment, I went straight to the chamber of my wife.

Without being deficient in moral courage, I am not a boisterous man. I do not boast of an eye like Mars, to threaten and command, or glory in producing a shudder with the creaking of my shoes. I mention this to show that my manner, though rebuking, was not intended to be severe. To awe by my authority, and soothe by my condescension, was the design; but even in this limited effort I am conscious of a lamentable failure.

Seated upon the floor, within an airy castle of dry-goods, whose battlements of flannel and linen cambric frowningly encircled her, was Malinda Jane. Before it, like an investing army, with colors flying, and a face radiant with defiant triumph, was Mrs. Mountchessington Lawk. She had complacently opened the siege with the mixture of a hot gin-toddy. My appearance upon this warlike scene was the signal for a salute both loud and watery (in short, tearful), entered into with a mutual heartiness by besieger and besieged. It was, moreover, rendered impressive by a waving spoon, which Mrs. Mountchessington Lawk moved solemnly backward and forward in a warning, funereal manner, as though protesting against some appalling fate. That she was in possession of my apartment, if not my house, I instinctively realized. She sat bolt upright, firm and strong as a Hindoo idol on its altar; a nebulous glare invested her head with a halo, through which bristling hair-pins stuck out in all directions, like lightning-rods with fitfully luminous points. The crystal wall of spectacles that bridged her nose seemed graven with the cabalistic words, "I've got you." A feeling of conscious guilt, of what an enfeebled mind failed to grasp, succumbed to the shock.

From amid the joint chorus of sobs and tears which burst forth with the wail of a Scottish slogan or an Indian death-song, I heard—

"Oh, my poor darling! Oh, my poor dear angel! Oh, Mr. Butterby, how *could* you?"

"Madam," I inquired, in amazement, "how could I what?"

It may be well to state the endearing epithet was applied to Malinda Jane.

"Oh, dear! dear! and all this time she has been scrimping and saving, I was unconscious as a child unborn. Cruel, *cruel* man!"

Mrs. Lawk, burying her hand in the depths of her pocket, drew forth an attenuated handkerchief, and carefully wiped her eyes.

"Please, ma——" interrupted Malinda Jane.

"Never, *never* again shall you leave my protecting wing. Oh, inhuman monster, how *could* you be so heartless?"

"Monster" was given with a decidedly unpleasant bite, and recalled my calmness.

"Mrs. Mountchessington Lawk," I placidly observed, "I have not the remotest idea what you are talking about."

"Moses Butterby, you're a brute."

She rose to her feet. A bundle, which, during the excitement, lay on her lap, broke open; and my mother-in-law, like Cleopatra in her roses, stood knee-deep in baby-clothes. In a moment the truth burst upon me. I was unmanned, limp, and disjointed. The shock was too much! A baby Butterby!

It is needless for me to remark to married men that the era of prospective paternity is an era of sacrifice. Why, in this time-honored custom, so much depends on one's mother-in-law, is a mystery I never could unravel. I look upon it as one of the unaccountable fatalities of man, to be placed in the category of grievances with prickly heat. Let it not be understood that my conduct was absolutely lamb-like. It was not until solemnly assured the visit would not be prolonged an unnecessary hour that I finally yielded. I think during that time I had a meaner opinion of my own importance than at any other period of my life. My domestic career resembled that of a child guilty of an irreparable wrong and tolerated only through dire necessity. Indeed, had Mrs. Mountchessington Lawk been a modern Rachel, and I the ruthless destroyer of her household, her conduct toward me could not have exhibited more injured resignation. I somehow grew to *feel* guilty, and it was only at rare intervals I mustered courage to look either her or Malinda Jane in the face.

The anticipated addition to the family brought an immediate addition to our furniture. The way the chairs multiplied was marvelous, and the number of sofas that accumulated in our parlor would have been gratifying to a Grand Turk. We suddenly grew plethoric in wash-stands, and appeared to possess armoires and bureaus in quantities and varieties sufficient (as the advertisements say) to suit the most fastidious taste. Even the bath-room did not seem to be neglected, and a modest effort was made to furnish the back gallery. One day I was astonished to find in the hall two hat-racks, and was nearly knocked down by the end of a great four-post bedstead that followed me in. I turned on the intruder, and discovered the little cobbler, apparently as much under the influence of liquor as on the day of his previous eccentricity, stupidly endeavoring to push one post in the door while the other bade fair to thrust itself through the ventilator. It was then I learned that in the array consisted the entire household treasures of Mrs. Mountchessington Lawk.

I may here mention that the cobbler had contracted a chronic habit of hanging around my back gate, but slunk away whenever I happened to observe him.

Gradually (leaving out the patients) our house began to wear the aspect of a hospital. The doctor made his appearance three times daily. An aged, red-faced nurse, smelling strong of whisky, wandered about like a disembodied spirit; and a lively young woman, her assistant, clattered up and down stairs at all hours of the day and night. Had the entire city concluded to multiply and replenish, the preparations could not have been on a grander scale.

Of the exact particulars of the event, I fear I am not altogether clear. I have an indistinct recollection of battling with a midnight thunder-storm, in a hopeless search for our medical man, and that, immediately on my return, that functionary (who had arrived during my absence) dispatched me on an equally important errand.

I remember pulling a great many night-bells and arousing an unlimited number of apothecaries; but the only act at all fresh in my recollection was slinking in the back gate at three o'clock A.M. (I had been locked out the front way), and finding the little cobbler, and a surrounding crowd of damp newsboys, cheering lustily for "Jinny." The cause of that commotion was also a mystery; but, when I entered the house, Master Moses Alphonso Butterby feebly echoed their shout of triumph.

Under different auspices, my paternal affection might have developed rapidly; but really, during the first few weeks of Moses Alphonso's existence, our intercourse was so exceedingly limited I scarcely knew him. Any intrusion within his little horizon of flannel or atmosphere of paregoric was so severe a tax on the nerves of Mrs. Lawk, that, out of consideration for her feelings, I rather avoided it. Indeed, had it not been for the activity of that eminently respectable lady, I would have fancied Moses Alphonso a brother-in-law instead of a son.

Bolted in by flannel bandages, barred with a cambric shirt, locked up in towels, imprisoned in petticoats, and finally incarcerated in a dungeon of wrappers and shawls,—from the first he had the appearance of an unhappy little convict. Mrs. Lawk invariably acted as chief jailer, and, taking him into custody, changed his various places of confinement with the austerity of a keeper of the Tower. My own position hourly became more ambiguous; indeed, had it not been for the monthly bills, I would have scarcely believed myself possessed of a house at all. I impatiently awaited the promised evacuation; and when Moses Alphonso reached his third birthday (babies have these interesting periods monthly instead of annually) I ventured a hint that our own furniture was ample for all requirements.

To my despair, Mrs. Lawk had rented her house. Malinda Jane's confinement (which in my simplicity I imagined was of short duration), it seemed, had been protracted from the day of her marriage.

Society was essential to her happiness; and society Mrs. Lawk was determined she should have. If through her illness my privileges experienced curtailment, her recovery brought annihilation itself. Notwithstanding my piteous petition, we suddenly expanded into eminent gentility.

I am dimly conscious that to many of our guests my introduction was to Mrs. Lawk a poignant mortification. Most of them I never did know. Several, however, seemed invited for my especial benefit; and this piece of malignity will never cease to harrow.

How could *I* talk to Miss Rose Buddington Violet, when she let down her back hair and made eyes at the moon? *I* had no back hair (in fact, none at all to speak of), and scarcely knew there *was* a moon.

When Mrs. Jesse Hennessee of Tennessee (whose husband is interested in iron) persisted in making a blast-furnace of the kitchen stove, what could I say?

There was Miss Aurelia Wallflower, who believed the world hollow, and dolls stuffed with saw-dust, continually expatiating on the sufferings of early Christians. *I* have never read Fox's Book of Martyrs. With Mrs. Lucretia McSimpkins I had some relief. She was fond of operatic music, and, it is true, banged our piano out of tune at every visit,—indeed, her efforts resembled a boiler-maker's establishment under full headway; but, when she did subside, her perfect and refreshing silence lasted for hours.

Malinda Jane, for whose amusement all this was designed, did not seem more enthusiastic than myself. Most of her time was spent in a corner, staring confusedly at the assembled company, and contemplating in silent amazement the volubility of her respected parent.

In addition to toning down my exuberance with the softening influence of ladies' society, Mrs. Lawk decided on a course of restriction. My allowance of clean linen suddenly diminished one-half and under no circumstances was I to presume to take a fresh pocket-handkerchief more than once in two days. She changed the dinner-hour, and declared supper (except for Malinda Jane, poor dear!) strictly prohibited. For a time I mitigated the last grievance by eating oysters; but, an unlucky burst of confidence having divulged the dissipation, a solemn lecture on my duty to my family was its quietus. Every article of food was put under lock and key, the night-latch was changed, and

Mrs. Lawk, in addition to her duties as jailer to Master Moses Alphonso, constituted herself turnkey of the establishment. The parlor, except when we "received," was declared forbidden ground: her dismay at finding my papers there, one evening, was perfectly heart-rending. There was a sudden inquiry concerning my loose change, and I was furnished with a memorandum-book in which to write down my daily disbursements. Frequent visits to the opera (oh, the torture of those evenings!) had been an invariable rule with the Mountchessingtons; and, at the risk of rendering impotent the tympanum of both ears, I was compelled to continue that respectable custom. Persons occupying our position should be careful with whom they associated; and the character of my companions underwent a severe investigation. She even interfered with my business, and declared the soap brokerage (one of my most lucrative departments) utterly beneath a gentleman. One by one my little personal comforts faded away. Symptoms of annoyance, persistently repeated, whenever I took off my coat or put on my slippers, kept me at all times prepared for the streets. Cabbage (a favorite dish) was quietly discarded from the dinner-table. My library was turned into a nursery for Master B.

The mute, unresisting manner in which I surrendered my fading glory was surprising. I was appalled in contemplating it; I am breathless now with indignation in referring to it. In short, like Daniel and the Hebrew children, I went up through much tribulation; but my deliverance (oh, how I daily and hourly thank Divine Providence for that blessed moment!) was at hand.

It was the evening of an election for an alderman, I think; but, as in our retired portion of the city none but the lowest vagabonds gave politics a thought, there was comparatively no excitement. Mrs. Lawk, from the wide circle of society in which she moved, had invited a goodly number to an entertainment. Even our inordinate supply of sofas were filled, and scarcely a chair in the house remained unoccupied. In a rash moment I asked two or three of my own cronies; but not many minutes elapsed ere both my companions and myself were made to feel the folly of the temerity.

Ignorant of dancing, unskilled in whist or the art of polite conversation, we were terminating our third hour of judicious snubbing in a corner. Mrs. McSimpkins had just concluded a battle-piece of great length and power, when the rehearsal of our shuddering comments was suddenly banished by the deafening roll of a drum. I rushed to the window, and, to my horror, discovered a torchlight procession halted immediately in front of the house. Perhaps a hundred men, in all stages of political enthusiasm and intoxication, surrounded by a crowd of wretched women and girls, waved their lights with demoniac frenzy, and, apparently through a common throat, gurgled three hideous cheers. There was a charge of Mrs. Lawk's friends to the windows, and then a stampede to the back parlor. In vain I expostulated; idly I insisted on my utter lack of interest in the questions of the day: the political party *would* come in, and how was I to prevent it? The absence of embarrassment and amiable indifference to form that characterized the intrusion was something unique. There was a difference in shape and mode of wearing, about the hats, really refreshing, and a variety of quality and nauseousness in the cigars everybody smoked, that, if anything, added zest to the scene.

Boots unconscious of the existence of a door-mat speedily graced the hall-floor with a perfect cushion of mud. Their wearers, rapidly dividing into groups, plunged into earnest conversation concerning the events of the day. The candid manner in which my own character was discussed, and their frankness in touching on my peculiarities, was not the least gratifying feature of the visit. In the course of two or three minutes, one would have supposed my residence a political club-room, and my uninvited guests in the peaceful enjoyment of their inalienable rights.

At length there was a cry of "Here he is! here he is!"

Every window on the square went up, and the neighborhood suddenly whitened with night-capped heads. I heard a crash of glass, and felt convinced that this time the ventilator had gone for certain. There was a fresh rush from the street, and, finally, seated on a shutter (borne on the shoulders of four stout men) and complacently swinging his legs, appeared the little cobbler. A radiant joy in his face, and a knowing wink in his eye, told plainly the combined influence of triumph and unlimited libation. Reeling profoundly to the assembled company, and casting a drunken leer at Mrs. Lawk, he exclaimed, "Mary Ann,—'s—no use, I'm—'s—good—as—he—is. I'm—an (hic)—an—Alderman. Butterby—embrace—your poor ol'—father—'n—law."

Of the conclusion of this episode, I fear I am somewhat confused. I have an indistinct recollection that Mrs. Lawk and Malinda Jane were both carried off in a fainting condition; and that my enthusiastic friends gave three rousing cheers for Alderman Lawk, and three more for me. I remember my father-in-law insisted on holding a meeting then and there and nominating me for Governor. His constituents considered the idea most judicious, and warmly applauded it. Mrs. Lawk's friends disappeared precipitately through the back way, amid renewed sounds of crashing glass and breaking china, while I hovered around the unterrified Democracy of the —— ward, earnestly beseeching them to go into the street. My efforts were at last crowned with success. I was left alone amid the wreck of my household gods; but for an hour afterward, as I lay cowering on the sofa, I could hear disconnected speeches from my door-steps, encouraged from time to time with tremendous cheers for Lawk, cheers for Butterby, and cheers for "Jinny." The same general mystification and uncertainty regarding my actions pervaded the entire night; but morning brought relief, and in more ways than one. Mrs. Lawk had disappeared, and her chattels were following. The victory was as sudden as it was unexpected.

Who would have thought that out of this storm of mortification was to spring the bow of promise? The day after witnessed the exit of my most respected mother-in-law and her amiable husband, for Cheyenne City; from which place we have recently heard from them as ornamenting the first Comanche and Blackfeet circles.

Her reason for concealing the relationship was never developed. Indeed, I was too much overcome with joy ever to inquire. Undisturbed by discordant elements, the fires of matrimonial affection burning as brightly as when lighted upon my marriage morn, I now calmly survey the re-establishment of a happy household, over which reign domestic bliss and—Master Moses Alphonso Butterby.

Such is an accurate statement of the case, all of which is respectfully submitted.

FOOTNOTES:

[A] For many useful hints in this diagnosis, Mr. Butterby is indebted to Mr. E.C. Hancock, of New Orleans.

DIAMONDS AND HEARTS.

A Sketch of Rio de Janeiro.

CHAPTER I.

The sun was setting on the Passeio Publico. On one side the fading light gilded the delicate green of the palms, and on the other it shimmered on the placid waters of the bay.

It whitened the little lodges, nestling in the luxuriance of foliage, and glistened on the gaudy boats, lying motionless on the pearly bosom of the deep. It sparkled on the little lakes where troops of joyous children gathered around the swans, and lost itself in the blue mists that circled the green and purple mountains in the distance.

Past the clustered giants of the sea, whose banners told of mighty nations that made war, past the forts where the sentries kept weary pace on the ramparts, it lighted up the "Pão de Assucar;" through the crowded thoroughfares where the hum of traffic told of multitudes in peace, it glowed on the Corcovado.

Far into the golden west, past the islands that dotted the harbor, past the last villa of São Christovão, it burned and blazed among the hills, until shadowy peaks, that seemed but ghosts in the dim remoteness, burst resplendent on the view, gorgeous in their prodigality of color.

Rio de Janeiro had mustered her children in crowds. Long and broad as was the promenade, its marble mosaics scarce contained room for the multitude. Anxious matrons, on one side, gathered on the granite stairs to watch their children in the garden beneath; heedless youngsters, on the other, hung over the balustrades for a view of the tide swelling at the foot of the wall; fair young *donnas*, bewildered at the throng of admirers, filled the air with peals of glad laughter; exquisite *senhors*, thrilled by the music, yielded themselves willing captives to the seductive influences of the hour.

Who but a Latin can understand the wild abandon of a *festa*? who but he can enter into the spirit of the many fête-days sanctioned by his ancient Church?

Armand Dupleisis, in his seat over the sea, stared absently at the jocose revelers, for he was a stranger in a strange land. He leaned back on the granite railings with the easy indolence of an invalid, though his frame was robust and sinewy as a mountaineer's. The hidden power of his bronzed and Moresque features, if developed, might inspire a certain amount of wonder; but *then* you would as readily have sought expression in the statues below. His gaze was almost indifferent; yet the unmoving eyes took a mental inventory of everything. Had their owner been provided with a memorandum-book and a stubby pencil, the catalogue could not have been more complete.

Among the hundreds present, those eyes picked out one man and one woman. They followed them in their rambles through the dome-roofed shelters; they scrutinized them as they lingered near the band; they searched them out when mingled with the throngs on the promenade. They did not seem to be watching, but they were; and their owner did not look interested, but he was.

The man, physically speaking, was a marvel; but there was an air of foppish elegance in his movements, and a silky kind of beauty, like that of a leopard. His head was small, but finely formed, and covered with flossy hair black as ebony. His features, though clearly cut, wore, from their extreme delicacy, an almost feminine expression. His hands were small and exquisitely shaped; his mustache curled gracefully from his lip; and, when speaking, he bit the ends of it in a nervous, almost embarrassed way.

The woman was a proud, passionate daughter of the sun. The brown blood of the sun burned in her veins, and the soul of the sun streamed shaded from her eyes. A sumptuous splendor mingled, moist and languid, with their light. She was clothed in the sunlight. It glistened in the soft darkness of her hair; it glowed in the rubies that clung to her swelling throat; it flashed on her robe tremulous with radiance. From a coquettish little hat a long white plume fluttered over her curls, and a floating cloud of fleecy under-sleeve half concealed an arm of snowy purity. Her life, though in its spring, seemed goldened with the flush of summer; her morning flashed with the meridian luster of perfect day; and yet the eyes that scanned so closely remained undazzled. Their owner had heard of her, and of her conversation, sparkling with wit and humor and mocking irony; but he was not fascinated. He saw but a woman for whom no surprises appear to survive. What see we?

Were you to question the crowd, they would tell you the man was Edgar Fay; that, years before, his father brought him, a velvet-coated boy, to Rio de Janeiro; that shortly afterward he died, leaving the son and a baby sister a small fortune; that the sister, being under the control of a mother who had deserted her husband, was never heard of; and that the guardians, finding no coheir, had spent the money on Edgar's education, afterward securing him a position under the Imperial government.

About the woman they would say, "She is Mademoiselle Milan, just arrived on the French packet, to fill an engagement as leading lady at the *Alcasar*."

Concerning Dupleisis, except that he had arrived recently on the English steamer, that he seemed to be a man of leisure, and paid promptly for what he received, they could tell you nothing.

The glowing sunshine faded entirely out of the sky, the thick-walled houses flickered faintly through their staring casements, the lamps on the streets glimmered dismally at the returning crowds, and one by one the lights began to quiver on the water. The Passeio, an hour before too cramped for the multitude, was now deserted; but Dupleisis, nothing daunted, smoked on. Disgusted at the necessity which compelled his presence, and annoyed at the stupidity of the few people he had met, he commented savagely on their peculiarities, and anathematized with merciless ingenuity.

"Pshaw, M. Dupleisis! you are only angry because you cannot have chicken-pie every day for dinner. What have the Brazilians done to you?"

Dupleisis gazed at the speaker in astonishment.

"Their impudence, rather than degeneracy, perhaps should surprise."

"Really, M. Dupleisis! I fear you are a cynic. In the gayest promenade in the empire, you are filled with violence. You are a spoiled child looking in at a shop-window and admiring nothing. Are you going to cry with a mouth *full* of sugar-plums?"

"Pardon me," said the Frenchman, haughtily, "but it is an awkward habit of mine to feel curious concerning the *names* of my associates."

"Let me hasten to enlighten you:—Percy Reed, diamond-dealer, Rua do Ouvidor, at your service. You brought me a letter of introduction; but, unluckily, I was out of town when you arrived."

The dark eyes glanced at the speaker closely as they had watched the man and the woman. There was something in the face that commanded respect. The broad high forehead, the eyes flashing with scornful mirth, and the thin lips curling with such a whimsical mixture of kindliness and sarcasm, bespoke a man of mind. Since reaching Rio, Dupleisis had searched for these three, and he liked this one the best. Reed took out his eye-glass, and, adjusting it carefully on his nose, surveyed Dupleisis deliberately from head to foot.

"You'll do," he remarked, after some little thought; "but I still believe that in your bread-and-butter days some friend thought you sarcastic. I knew a young girl once who was told she had a musical laugh, and the consequence was she giggled the rest of her life. Now, if you don't wish to see us locked in here for the night, come along."

CHAPTER II

The establishment of Percy Reed, diamond-dealer, Rua do Ouvidor, was a corner-building, almost the exact counterpart of a dozen edifices on the same square. The basement was of polished blocks of black and white marble, and the upper portion faced with blue and white porcelain tiles. From above, the front rooms looked out through bow-windows at small balconies with brass-knobbed railings and thick glass floors; those in rear looked through glass doors at a flat roof, one story high, paved with black and white marble squares. This breathing-place of the household was adorned with pots of flowers and evergreens and provided with neat iron chairs. It was divided from the breathing-place of the adjoining household by a low brick wall.

Below, pedestrians gazed in through rose-wood doors and French plate windows. The counting-room had rather the appearance of an elegant boudoir than of a place of business. The floor was of alternate strips of satin-wood and ebony; the walls and ceiling were paneled with rose-wood, and rows of small glistening show-cases contained samples of the dazzling gems. In the rear—but so covered with the glossy finish as to be almost imperceptible—was a huge vault, containing precious stones of a value almost sufficient to change the fate of an empire. Farther back, and opening on the side street, was a long, dark hall-way, from which a winding staircase led to the residence above. The second floor of the adjoining house was usually let furnished to members of the dramatic profession; and on this occasion it was occupied by Mademoiselle Adrienne Milan, of the *Alcasar*.

The day after the *festa*, the lady, in a simple morning toilet, had moved her table and sewing-chair into the open air. Instead of sewing, she was occupied in furbishing up some old stage jewelry, and her visitor, stretched on an iron bench, calmly puffed a cigar. From his manner, one would imagine him master rather than guest; but that Mademoiselle Milan and a female servant were the sole occupants there is not a doubt.

With the utmost nonchalance, he had ordered a pillow, and, his ambrosial locks buried in its soft depths and his feet raised high above his head, he lounged a modern Apollo, scrutinizing with supercilious indifference the lady's work. If the cigar-ashes at his side were a criterion, he had been lying there for hours; and if the nervous movements of Mademoiselle were significant, he had been lying there an hour too long. For some minutes the silence was broken only by the jingle of the gaudy ornaments, and then the man exclaimed, "But, *ma chère* Adrienne, I am short—deuced short. Delay is ruin. How am I to live?"

"Work," said the lady, curtly.

"There you are again, with your cursed woman's wisdom! What are you here *for*? What am *I* here for?"

Mademoiselle answered, with a shrug, "Judging from your position, I would say, to enjoy your ease; from your language, to annoy me."

He raised himself to a sitting posture. "Adrienne Milan, do you take me for an idiot?"

"Edgar Fay, you are insulting."

"Prima donnas of the *Alcasar* are not usually so sensitive," broke out the visitor, with a laugh.

The woman sprang to her feet, and in the haste overturned the table with its glittering baubles.

"Go! go!" she fiercely exclaimed. "The compact between you and me is sacred. Another word, and I reveal all."

White as any ghost, he started up, and, without uttering a sound, slunk away.

Trembling with rage and mortification, Mademoiselle Milan sunk into a seat; but hers was not a nature to dwell long on trouble. With a woman's spirit of order, she commenced picking up the finery scattered around her, and putting it away. Among other things was a box of quartz diamonds, which, being small, flew in all directions. All within view were collected, and she turned to go.

"There are several lying near that flower-pot in the corner."

The lady looked up. Standing on a chair on the other side, and leaning lazily over the wall, was Armand Dupleisis.

CHAPTER III.

"Has Flora proved more attractive than Thalia?"

Armand Dupleisis, long since become acquainted, stood examining a bouquet of roses and geraniums in the music-room of Mademoiselle Milan, and the lady was seated near him, trifling with the keys of her piano.

"I gaze on beauty, mademoiselle, to accustom my eyes to divinity."

"Really! Were it not for his gigantic proportions, one would suppose man was reared in an atmosphere of compliment."

"You mistake us. Though not a favorite diet, in Pekin we devour rice with the gusto of the most polished Celestial."

"I bow to your sincerity. Women, then, are to be talked to of birds, and flowers, and stars, and fed on water-cresses?"

"Women, mademoiselle, make men apt scholars in the art of pleasing. I have studied much."

"How singular!" rejoined the lady. "I should never have detected it."

"True art, mademoiselle, lies in its concealment. My life has been one of concealment."

"Now you pique my curiosity," she replied. "Do let me learn the 'veritable historie.'"

The smile on Mademoiselle Milan's face showed that the interest was feigned, but the grim look about Dupleisis' mouth proved him conscious of it. A man without an object would have changed the subject at once; but Dupleisis *had* an object, and did not.

"I was ushered into this land of hope and sunny smiles with scarcely any other patrimony than a name."

"What limited resources!" ejaculated the lady, with a slight sneer.

"While blushing with the consciousness of my virgin cravat, I went to Paris, that sacred ark, which saves from shipwreck all the wretched of the provinces if but crowned with a ray of intellect."

"And which saved you, of course," continued the lady.

"Through the influence of my friends, I entered the *École Polytechnique*, and, after graduating, cut the army, and cast my fate, for better or for worse, in the flowery paths of literature."

"Now, do not say it proved for worse."

"It was for worse," said Dupleisis. "My family were treated shabbily; 'the muse is a maiden of good memory,' but a *cocote*; my satiric efforts were rewarded by a *lettre de cachet*."

"What a loss to France!"

"At the accession of the Emperor, I returned, a prodigal son of Mars, and now manage to sustain myself by———"

"By writing sonnets to Brazilian hospitality," interrupted mademoiselle.

Dupleisis bowed gravely. "Anxious to do so, mademoiselle, but I have not, as yet, collected sufficient material."

The retort crimsoned the lady's face, and Dupleisis adroitly covered her confusion by asking her to sing.

"What will you say to me, when you speak of yourself as though you were a block of wood?"

"The prosy geologist talks pedantically of a granite rock, and is mute when he sees the flower that blooms above it."

"*Mon Dieu*, M. Dupleisis! I cannot sit by and hear *Chamfort* so ruthlessly robbed."

"Mademoiselle, you are unkind. I say nothing complimentary but you cry, 'Stop thief!'"

The lady played a few sparkling bars, and sang. She had a magnificent voice, but her music, like herself, was studied, faultless, but chilling as the north wind. It swelled deep and full, in rich, flute-like tones, now ringing clear and sweet in pure, rippling notes, now quivering low in waves of enchanting melody. There were soft, gurgling sounds, that flowed wild and free as a mountain-rivulet. It was brilliant, bewildering; but the dazzle was like the frozen glitter of an icicle. Suddenly, a look of unmitigated scorn swept across her face, and the music ceased.

She eyed Dupleisis for a moment half defiantly, and asked, "Would you really like to hear me sing?"

Dupleisis answered, earnestly, "Yes."

A plaintive prelude followed, and her voice mingled with it almost imperceptibly. It was one of those gloomy Spanish ballads, dramatic rather than harmonious, that poured forth its mournful strains in the fitful measure of an Æolian harp. There were bursts of pathos that seemed to echo from her very soul. It was fierce, mocking, passionate; tender, wicked, terrible. It sank in sobs of melting compassion; it implored pity and sympathy in words of thrilling entreaty; and then it rose, cold and calm, in sounds of withering derision and implacable hate. It trembled, it scorned, it pleaded, it taunted, it struggled, it hoped, it despaired; and then, as if for the dead, it wailed and died in a long, helpless cry of sorrow.

Dupleisis sat listening to the dreary history entranced. There was love, and feeling, and fond womanly devotion; there was refined thought, gentle pity, and warm generous charity; and there was a neglected heart, a gloomy, embittered mind, a life lost in utter desolation. The glorious being whom God had created to cheer and encourage man was a beautiful statue.

Who would teach that heart to feel again? Who turn to quivering flesh that rigid marble? Yet the man of iron sat masking his features, controlling his emotions, with every muscle under his command. It was a flash of real feeling from a proud, sensitive woman, but it passed lightly as a snowdrift on a frozen river.

CHAPTER IV.

"Mr. Reed, you certainly are the most old-maidish man I ever saw in my life."

The room did appear old-maidish, as Mademoiselle Milan stood looking in. The balmy breeze fluttered pleasantly past the little French curtains, the glowing sunshine warmed the delicate tracery of the walls and lighted up the flowers on a huge rug spread on the bare floor. A tiny bouquet of Spanish violets, in a wonderful little vase, filled the room with a dreamy perfume, such as one sometimes imagines he would find in those far-off little islands in the South seas. There were crayon sketches hung between the windows, here and there a statuette filled a niche, and out on the glass-floored gallery was a perfect bower of flowers. There were several easy-chairs placed about in comfortable positions, as if they were all made to sit on, and a great lounge, covered with green marine, stood, like a small grass-mound, under one of the windows.

Percy Reed, seated near a table loaded with needle-books, silk-winders, and a hundred little trinkets, with a cigar in his mouth, and a sock, with a little round gourd shoved into the foot of it, in his hand, was intently occupied in darning a hole in the toe.

"There! don't throw away your cigar. *Mon Dieu!* can a person never see you without being overpowered at your grand politeness?"

"Mademoiselle, I make no apologies. Buttons will come off, and stockings will contract holes. Washer-women are heartless. The mountain will not come to Mahomet: therefore I darn 'em myself."

"A philosopher under all circumstances. And pray what have you done with your pupil in morality and economy?"

"Oh, Dupleisis? I have started him out in a carriage to view the wonders of this 'River of January.' By-the-by, if you ever hope to attract, don't dream of mentioning figures in the presence of our mysterious Frenchman."

"Why?"

"The branch of mathematics known as simple addition seems to be the crowning glory of his intellect. He knows to a *milreis* the value of this building, from chimney-pot to cellar."

"Blessed with curiosity," said Mademoiselle, significantly.

"Mathematics entirely. If Armand Dupleisis were entering the pearly gates of Paradise, amid the resounding hallelujahs of cherubim and seraphim, he would deliberately count the cost of the entire wardrobe, before he thought of receiving the waters of eternal life."

"Mr. Reed," said Mademoiselle, earnestly, "who *did* you ever see of whom you *could* not speak lightly?"

"One person in the world—my mother. Sometimes in my dreams of the 'auld lang syne' I almost see that dear little lady; she had a window just like that, with the foliage rustling over it just as this does. Never, mademoiselle, does that little morning-wrapper come up before my eyes without making me a better and a purer man."

Both were silent for some minutes after this. Mademoiselle Milan sat leaning her face against the crimson lining of her chair, apparently lost in thought.

At length she said, "Would to God that all men understood women as well as you!"

"But *your* mother; where is she, mademoiselle?"

The lady's face turned as pale as marble, and her little white hands grasped the arms of her chair, until they seemed almost imbedded in the ebony. She attempted an utterance, but her voice failed her, and there was a dead silence.

Reed was a man of feeling. He did not talk, nor persuade her to talk. He did not even sit doing nothing. He went out on the balcony to examine the flowers. He climbed noiselessly up the lattice-work for jasmines fluttering in the evening breeze. Finally, he took up a violin and played.

He always played well, but now the music was low and soft,—old Scotch ballads, wild and mournful, touching little German songs, plaintive romances full of subdued passion. Mademoiselle Milan did not notice him; but in her heart she felt grateful for his consideration. Gradually the color returned to her face, and, soothed by the sad, sweet strains, she sunk into dreamy reverie.

"When we have reached another sphere, where emotion governs instead of thought, I think that man will speak in splendid music."

Reed looked at her earnestly for a moment, and then said, "Mademoiselle, why did you never write?"

"The public treats authors very much as drill-sergeants do recruits,—drunk the first day, and beaten the rest of their lives."

"Great minds *rule* the public."

"And yet I fear your courage would ooze away when you came to lay a lance at rest against such a windmill as the common sense of the nineteenth century, whirling its rotary sails under the steady breeze of ridicule. I am a woman, and know a woman's place. I have had dreams in my time,—'dreams like that flower that blooms in a single night, and dies at dawn;' but they are passed. You see, I carry the glare of the foot-lights even here." And a bitter smile curled from her lip.

"Mademoiselle," said Percy, solemnly, "the foot-lights enable you to move man to a hundred passions."

"Yes; it reduces me to the level of a harlequin, to be laughed with, and laughed *at*. Who are *my* friends? Are they the idle boys who send me bouquets and never mention my name without looking unutterable things? Have I no tastes, no likings, no feelings, no emotions? In the name of God, was I created only to memorize so many lines of Racine, Corneille, or Voltaire per diem?"

It was a tone of almost ferocity with which she spoke, and the trembling lip, the flashing eye, and the swollen veins on her temple betrayed the self-scorn racking her heart within her.

A bang at the hall-door, and heavy footsteps on the marble pavement, forced her to composure.

"Old-maidish to the last!" (the lady commenced picking the dead leaves off a geranium). "This geranium looks as if you had watched it a year; and this old gray hat, I suppose, you have hung above it for good luck."

"The hat belongs to a friend abroad, and is not to be moved until his safe return; but the geranium was presented not a week ago by my ever-faithful money. You see the magic charm. Here are careful watching, weeks of anxiety, and, no doubt, a modicum of affection (for I *have* heard people say they loved flowers), bartered away for one *milreis*."

"Apropos of money,—I thought I was to have a view of the treasures of Aladdin, locked up in the vaults below."

"Of a surety you shall."

Reed excused himself, and in a short time reappeared, bearing a large iron casket. Mademoiselle Milan's face turned a shade or two paler when she saw him; for he was accompanied by Edgar Fay. It had now become quite dark, and Percy Reed lighted the gas-jet before opening the casket. It was made in imitation of the ordinary iron safe, but opening at the top.

When the glare of the gas struck the dark recesses of the velvet lining, a gleam of radiance shot up that fairly dazzled. Great grains of light, large as peas, shimmered and glittered with an unearthly brilliancy. Blue, purple, violet, and a gorgeous white that combined the whole, sparkled in their turn with weird splendor. It looked like a flash from heaven turned suddenly on a startled world. Both Mademoiselle Milan and Fay stood breathless with astonishment, and it was many minutes before they regained their composure.

Hearing the heavy rumbling caused by the lowering of the iron shutters in the counting-room, Mademoiselle urged Mr. Reed to return the gems to the vault before it closed.

He assured her it was entirely unnecessary, saying that larceny was a crime unknown to Brazilians, and that he had provided for exigencies such as this. Moving the piles of thread and embroidery silk to the side of the table, he touched a spring, and a lid flew up. The table, though presenting the appearance of fragility itself, was really of iron, and contained a vault that would puzzle the most expert of burglars.

Just then Dupleisis called from the street, and both Reed and Edgar Fay went out on the gallery to see him. He had made arrangements to spend the night with a friend, and the three stood chatting for some minutes, the Frenchman giving an amusing description of his adventures among the *Brazileiros*.

Shortly afterward, Mademoiselle Milan and Fay took their leave. The wind by this time was blowing so fiercely that no taper could live in the gusts; so both were compelled to grope their way through the hall, which was dark as Erebus.

The door was faithfully bolted, and the casket carefully placed in the secret vault; but when Percy Reed awoke in the morning he found both open, and the diamonds, worth a million, missing.

CHAPTER V.

"Mademoiselle Milan, I wish you good-evening."

The lady bowed. She was reclining on a divan, before a large mirror, absently turning the rings on her finger; but in her simple négligée she appeared more beautiful than ever. The long, dark ringlets gave the oval face a look of earnestness, the fierce Italian blood glowed in her cheeks, and the flashing brilliancy of her eyes had a restlessness that was unusual. She was evidently suffering from nervous excitement; but there was a fascinating grace in every movement, and even in the easy indolence of her position.

"Take a seat on that sofa, by the side of my little dog. Is he not pretty?"

"Very," replied Dupleisis; "but I am more interested in his mistress. We have not met for a week,—not, in fact, since two thieves robbed Mr. Reed of a fortune."

Dupleisis said this with pointed significance; but the lady preserved the coolest unconcern.

"The muse of the foot-lights is the most jealous of mistresses."

"True," replied Dupleisis; "but in this case she has had rivals."

"I choose to amuse myself with a crowd, who eat my suppers and make me laugh."

"And among the jesters you number the Minister of War and Chief of Police."

"I may need their aid."

"Mademoiselle Milan, you *do* need their aid; but, with all your charming courtesies, you have not secured it."

"M. Dupleisis chooses to speak in enigmas. I am obtuse."

"At our last most agreeable *tête-à-tête*, you were pleased to feel interested in my somewhat sluggish history. Would you pardon a few inquiries concerning yours?"

"M. Dupleisis, I am at your service."

"Two months since, you resided in the Rue de Luxembourg, Paris."

"This is an assertion. I expected an inquiry."

Dupleisis took from a pocket-book a half-sheet of thin, closely-written letter-paper, and spread it out on the table before him.

"It was about two months ago that this document was blown from your window. Am I right, Mademoiselle Milan?"

"It *was* blown from my writing-desk into the street."

"I knew I was right; for 'twas I that picked it up. It is a letter, written in Rio de Janeiro, and contains the details of a plot to rob one of the wealthiest diamond-dealers in this city. You may think my interest singular, mademoiselle; but the merchant deals with every large jewelry-house in Paris. Their loss by a felony of this magnitude would be immense."

Mademoiselle Milan listened with an air of indifference that was absolutely freezing.

"You may think it singular, also, that when, shortly afterward, you started for Bordeaux, I went by the same train; and that when you concluded to prolong your journey to Brazil by the French packet, via Lisbon, it was *I* who assisted with your luggage."

"There is nothing low enough to be singular in M. Dupleisis."

"Mademoiselle Milan, one week ago you and Edgar Fay went into the hall-way of Mr. Reed's house together, and you went *out* alone. Denial is useless, for I *saw* you. If you remember, the door was banged violently, and it was you who did it. A careless servant locked him in. He opened the secret vault in that table, and abstracted diamonds worth a million. You were wise in courting the Minister of War and Chief of Police, but your passports have been stopped. No power under heaven can get you out of Rio."

For the first time her countenance changed, and she looked at Dupleisis with a smile of contemptuous pity.

"So I was not wrong in suspecting you to be an agent of the police. How strong an alloy of cunning exists in every fool! The man whom you believe to have stolen a million is my own brother. The letter which caused this display of sagacity was paid for out of my wretched weekly earnings. At the sacrifice of every *sou* I owned, I came here to thwart the plot it spoke of."

Dupleisis glanced at her with an incredulous sneer.

"He wrote to Paris for a woman to assist him,—what weaklings you men are!—and, utterly unable to prevent the larceny, I pretended to be his accomplice. While you were exposing your ill-breeding by coarse criticisms on a people in every way your superior, I substituted for the real diamonds the paste gems you were so particular in noticing. What was stolen is my property. Go back to Mr. Reed, and tell him his diamonds are bundled into an old hat that hangs on the wall of his sitting-room; and tell him, furthermore, it was I who put them there. I did court the favor of the Minister of War, but it was to put that man in the army. I have watched over him for years, and, by the blessing of God, I will watch over him to the end. He has never known me, nor will he——" Suddenly she turned livid, and nervously clasped her hands over her breast.

"M. Dupleisis, I regret my inability to be present at the Assembly; but, really, I am engaged."

Dupleisis looked at her in astonishment.

Edgar Fay, pale and trembling, was standing behind them. He must have heard every word; for he sunk helplessly and faint on the floor, hiding his face in the depth of his degradation.

Why should we follow them any further? *Can* I tell how the miserable man, cringing at the feet of that pure woman, narrated his dreary history of folly, extravagance, and dishonor? Need it be said that, through all his dissipation, frivolity, and crime, his gentle sister clung to him, and, smiling through her tears, bade him go and sin no more? She stole upon him like a shadow in the night, and, her labor of love ended, faded away. No entreaty of the generous diamond-dealer dissuaded her; no apology of the detective turned her from the one fixed purpose. The star of the *Alcasar* rose, culminated, and disappeared in two weeks.

O woman! I have seen you in the brilliant whirl of society, where all was gayety, gallantry, and splendor. I have seen your eyes flash triumphant, and daintily gaitered feet move fast and furious to the music of *les pièces d'or*. I have seen brave men stand fascinated at your side, and careless youth overflow the bumper of Johannisberger to health, and youth, and beauty. I have heard the stern cynic jingle his Napoleons in unison with the frantic strains, and sneer out, "*Vive la bagatelle!*" Daughters of marble! daughters of marble! Turn your snowy arms to the glittering gorgeous, scatter the golden heaps, deluge the world with champagne. Diamonds, *diamonds* must win hearts. I have watched you in a deeper, darker, madder whirl, while I have seen fair, blooming flowers wither in the hot hands of drunken licentiousness. Oh, Becky Sharp! Oh, *Dame aux Camellias*! you are but single dandelions in a parterre of heliotropes!

There was hurrying to and fro on the broad decks. Bustling cabin-boys rushed hither and thither with great baskets of stores; the jauntily-arrayed stewardess chatted saucily with her friends in the shore-boats; sailors slipped quietly over the bulwarks with their secretly-collected menageries of pets; watermen contended stoutly at the gangway for a landing near the steps; and dusky *cameradas* cursed, in broken French and Portuguese, at the weight of the trunks. Here a naturalist trembled with anxiety for the fate of a coral; there a bird-fancier worked himself into a small frenzy at the jostling of big parrots. Bones, fossils, plants, bottled fish, bananas, oranges, and mangoes, were mingled in one promiscuous heap. Monkeys of all tribes and shades of complexion, from the golden Mumasitte to the fierce Machaca, were crowded pell-mell into passages; and forcing them against the bulkheads were boxes of wine, jellies, and *doces* in their infinitesimal variety. Men and women, crouching in retired places, hurried through their few broken words of parting, and eyes were dried for the great heart-throb left for the very last. Off in the painted boats, ship-chandlers smilingly bowed their *bon voyage*, and faces pallid with grief gazed with swollen eyes at loved ones convulsed with emotion. The gorgeous custom-house officer has smoked his last cigarette and taken his last "dispatch;" the belated passenger, whose agonizing shrieks and spasmodic contortions finally attracted the attention of the captain, is at length, carpet-bag in hand, on board, and the sharp crash of the gong severs the lingering groups.

Who ever made an ocean voyage undismayed by the knell! It is the trumpet-tongue of reality, awakening the mind from the lethargy of its distress. The woe of separation, the terror of the journey, the vague apprehension of the future, meeting, burst upon you in the fullness of their stern reality. The bewildered mortal turns to gaze at the companions of his danger, casts a lingering look on those he has left behind; the groaning paddles, with reluctant plunges, begin their weary labor; the faces of the cheering crowd, one by one, drop out of the picture, until distance swallows the whole, and those nearer and dearer than all earth beside become a memory.

Far aft, under the waving tricolor, stood the woman of our story. Her fingers twined carelessly through the glittering necklace thrust into her hand as Percy Reed clambered into his boat, and her eyes rested sadly on an ungainly transport, already freighting with its cargo of mortality for the sacrifice at Humaita. The golden glow of the harbor was lost in the chilly mist; the bare mountain-tops loomed bleakly through the piles of cloudy haze. White waves curled dismally at the base of the Pão de Assucar, and the weird shrieks of the sea-gulls on the rocks that jutted around it made the dreariness more desolate. Far out in the trackless waste the sky lowered gloomily over the weary waters. Fit emblem of her path through life—dark was the picture, threatening the surroundings.

Pray for the woman doomed to a calling she cannot but despise! Pray for the being overflowing with good thoughts toward all mankind, sentenced to "tread the wine-press alone!" God have mercy upon us miserable sinners!

THE END.

Milton Keynes UK
Ingram Content Group UK Ltd.
UKHW030743071024
449371UK00006B/597